BEGINNING QIGONG

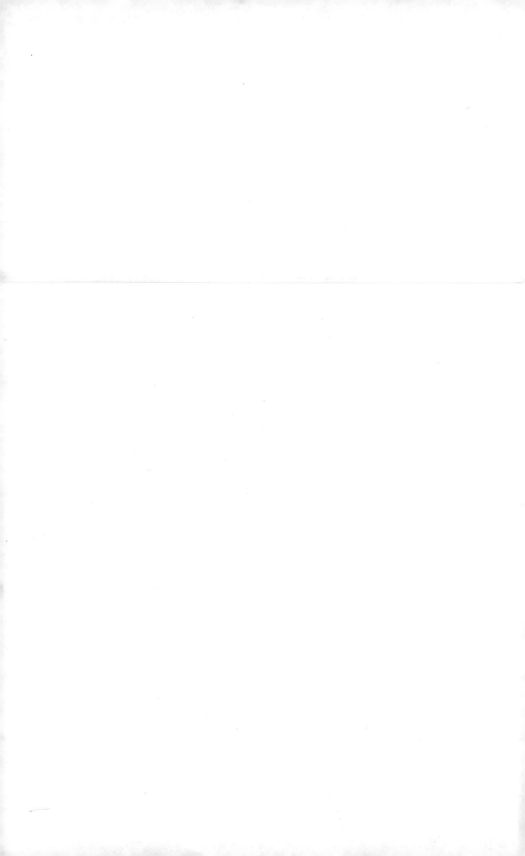

BEGINNING QIGONG
Chinese Secrets for Health and Longevity

Steven Kuei
and
Stephen Comee

CHARLES E. TUTTLE COMPANY
Rutland, Vermont & Tokyo, Japan

Disclaimer

Please note that the publisher of this instructional book is
NOT RESPONSIBLE in any manner whatsoever for any injury that may result
from practicing the techniques and/or following the instructions given within.
Since the physical activities described herein may be too strenuous in nature
for some readers, *it is essential that a physician be consulted prior to training.*

*Published by the Charles E. Tuttle Company, Inc.,
of Rutland, Vermont & Tokyo, Japan
with editorial offices at
Suido 1-chome, 2-6, Bunkyo-ku, Tokyo 112*

*First edition, 1993
Fourth printing, 1997*

*LCC Card No. 92-80691
ISBN 0-8048-1721-9*

PRINTED IN SINGAPORE

Contents

Introduction

WHAT IS QIGONG?

Qigong (pronounced "chee-goong") is a method of managing health that has been practiced since ancient times in China. It consists of a variety of techniques, some employing the breath, some acting on the outer muscles of the body, and others improving the operation of the various bodily systems. It is instrumental in the prevention and treatment of disease, the maintenance and improvement of health, and in holding back the process of aging and extending life. From ancient times, Qigong has been known as a method of eliminating disease and prolonging life.

In order to define the word "qigong," it is necessary to understand the concept woven into its two root words, *qi* and *gong*. *Qi* is written with the character that indicates the cooking and steaming of rice, and it is usually used to mean "air," "breath," or even "steam." But this is only the outer, external breath. The word *qi* is used by practitioners of Qigong and the martial arts to mean "internal *prana*," life force, or biopsychic internal energy. The canons of traditional Chinese medicine teach that life and health are a result of the harmonious flow of ample Qi throughout the body. When Qigong exercises are said to build up Qi, it is this internal Qi that they build up. All disease is thought to stem from a surplus or lack of, or disruption in the smooth flow of, this internal Qi. Acupuncture is based upon the belief that Qi circulates throughout the body along twelve major meridians, stimulation of which can cure various ailments.

The word *gong* means "effort," and is used in the word Qigong to indicate the diligent practice of exercises to help Qi to function properly and efficiently within the body. It is the true meaning of the word *gongfu* (usually spelled "kung-fu" in English), and refers not only to the duration and quality of one's Qigong practice, but also to the student's determination to learn the forms and practice them correctly, as well as to the later attainment of success through the building up of Qi. Thus, Qigong must be practiced with one's whole heart, sincerely, diligently, and with continuing perseverance. There should be no breaks in one's practice. This alone can affect the sought-after buildup of Qi.

It can be seen that the quality of one's Qigong practice has a direct effect upon the results one can attain. The purpose of doing these exercises is to foster and build up Qi, which involves three practices: 1) to breathe in and store vital Qi; 2) to maintain a calm state of mind; and 3) to keep the action of the bodily organs in harmony.

TECHNIQUES OF QIGONG

There are many systems involving Qigong techniques taught in China. They can be roughly divided into five categories: Taoist, Buddhist, Confucian, medical, and martial-arts related.

1. The principal aim of the Taoist method is to strengthen both body and mind, and through the constant use of Qigong techniques, to find "the elixir of immortality" and prolong life.

2. The Buddhist systems stress the control and tempering of the mind, and place little importance upon the bodily effects they produce.

3. The Confucian exercises emphasize regulating the mind and reaching a state of tranquility that gives rise to the cultivation of moral character.

4. The main purpose of the medical techniques is to cure diseases while promoting health and prolonging life.

5. The exercises taught within the various systems of martial arts are basically employed to build up the individual's inner strength such that he becomes invulnerable to both moral assault and actual physical attack. Although they also have the effect of preserving

health and prolonging life, they are principally practiced in order to help one to protect oneself with the self-defensive use of Qi in times of trouble.

Although all of these systems are different, they all fall into one of three types of Qigong: yin, or calm (Buddhist, Confucian); yin-yang, both passive and active (Taoist); and yang, or dynamic (medical, martial arts). But no matter which method of Qigong is employed, anyone who practices it diligently and with perseverance will succeed.

The techniques given in this book are a combination of those mentioned above, but they basically fall into the passive/active and dynamic types, as they are meant to build up bodily strength and prolong life.

HOW QIGONG CURES DISEASE

Chinese medicine has from ancient times postulated the existence of a network of channels through which Qi can flow to any part of the body. There are twelve major channels, or meridians, whose nature is described as either yin (calm) or yang (dynamic). Those connected to what are called "the solid organs" (the lungs, heart constrictor [pericardium], heart, spleen-pancreas, liver, and kidneys) and traveling along the interior lateral portions of the limbs are described as being of a yin nature; those connected to "the hollow organs" (the large intestine, triple warmer, small intestine, stomach, gall bladder, and urinary bladder) and traveling along the exterior portion of the limbs are described as being of a yang nature.

Note that when the Chinese refer to an "organ," they do not mean the physical organ described in Western medicine but the entire complex of bodily systems affected by and affecting that "organ." Thus, you will find above two "organs" unknown to Western science, the "heart constrictor," a complex system that controls the heart and its functions, and the "triple warmer," a tripartite system that controls the metabolism of the entire body.

Qi flows throughout the body in the order given in the table on the following page, starting in the lungs and moving through the other organs until it reaches the liver, whence it returns to the lungs and repeats its passage.

The twelve meridians are shown in Figures 1–12.

The Twelve Meridians

	Meridian	Location	Description
1.	Lung	Arm	Greater yin
2.	Large Intestine	Arm	Brilliant yang
3.	Stomach	Leg	Brilliant yang
4.	Spleen-Pancreas	Leg	Greater yin
5.	Heart	Arm	Lesser yin
6.	Small Intestine	Arm	Greater yang
7.	Urinary Bladder	Leg	Greater yang
8.	Kidney	Leg	Lesser yin
9.	Heart Constrictor	Arm	Absolute yin
10.	Triple Warmer	Arm	Lesser yang
11.	Gall Bladder	Leg	Lesser yang
12.	Liver	Leg	Absolute yin

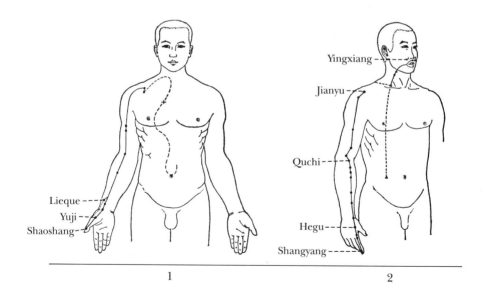

1   2

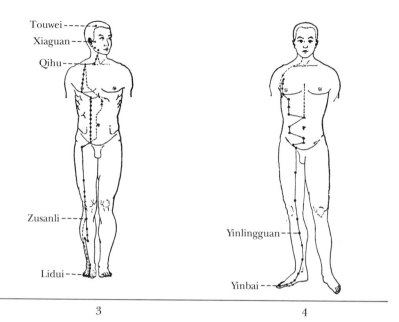

Touwei
Xiaguan
Qihu

Zusanli

Lidui

3

Yinlingguan

Yinbai

4

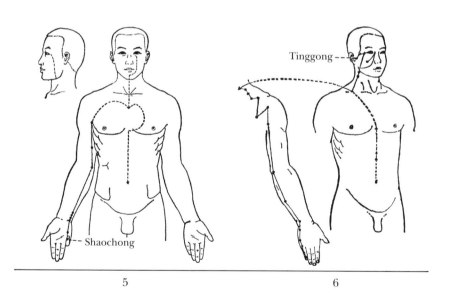

Shaochong

5

Tinggong

6

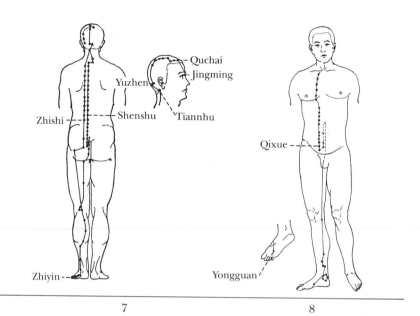

Quchai
Jingming
Yuzhen
Zhishi — Shenshu — Tiannhu
Qixue
Zhiyin
Yongguan

7   8

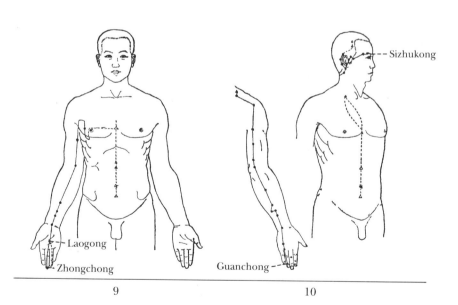

Sizhukong
Laogong
Zhongchong
Guanchong

9   10

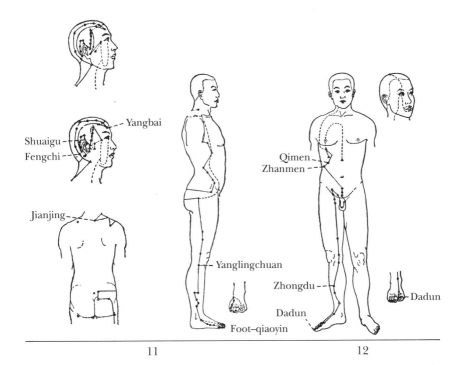

Shuaigu
Fengchi
Yangbai

Jianjing

Qimen
Zhanmen

Yanglingchuan

Zhongdu

Dadun

Dadun
Foot–qiaoyin

11   12

There are also eight special channels (Figs. 13–20) that are not connected with the internal organs, and through which Qi flows when there is enough build-up to overflow the twelve regular meridians. Thus, since Qi flows back into the twelve meridians when there is a deficiency of Qi in the body, the eight special channels serve as regulators for the twelve meridians. The movement of the Qi stored within these eight channels warms the internal organs and creates an inner heat that causes one to sweat. This is often seen in those who practice the internal martial arts such as T'ai-chi *(taiji-quan)*, Hsing-i *(xing'i-quan)*, and Pa-kua *(bagua-zhang)*.

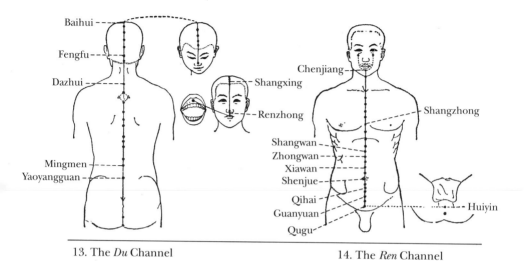

13. The *Du* Channel

14. The *Ren* Channel

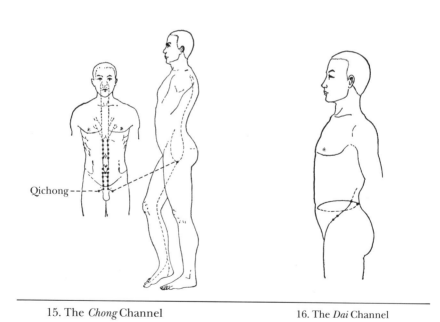

15. The *Chong* Channel

16. The *Dai* Channel

17. The *Yangqiao* Channel

18. The *Yingqiao* Channel

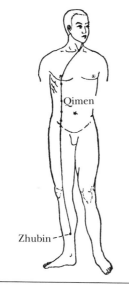

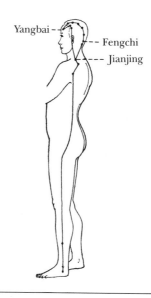

19. The *Yangwei* Channel

20. The *Yinwei* Channel

1

External Forms (Wai-gong)

PRINCIPLES

The Chinese have developed numerous external forms of exercise over the centuries. Among the three most popular of them, which can still be seen performed in parks in Asia in the early morning, are the Everyday Stretching Qigong (*Yijinjing,* lit.: muscle/bone-changing exercises), based upon the movements of farmers in growing and harvesting rice, which are included here; the Eight Brocade Exercises (*Baduanjin,* lit.: eight-section silk), which are not included, as they are already very popular in the West; and the Five Animal Forms (*Wuqinxi),* which are based upon animal movements and may be too difficult for beginners.

To perform these external forms correctly, practitioners must have the qualities of silk brocade; that is, they must be firm but supple, which is achieved by alternately tensing and relaxing the muscles. This is one of the most fundamental principles in all Chinese exercises, and has been found to be a great reliever of mental stress and bodily fatigue.

Another basic principle that all Chinese exercises share is concentration upon the lower abdomen. In Chinese medicine, this area is called the *dantian,* and is seen as the main storehouse of Qi, the life-force energy that flows throughout the body and maintains health. Qi can be stored up and then used in conjunction with the martial arts, giving greater power to the punches of masters who employ it.

Concentration upon the *dantian* is very conducive to relaxing the whole body, as it helps enhance the circulation of blood throughout the body; it also makes abdominal breathing a little easier and naturally shifts the body's center to a lower position, making the body's equilibrium more stable. Thus, if it is difficult for you to breathe abdominally, it is more important to focus upon the *dantian*, as the act of doing so will enable you to gradually shift from thoracic to abdominal breathing. In any case, the breathing should always be slow, even, and natural, as any irregularity of the breath will disrupt the natural flow of Qi.

In order for these exercises to have the maximum effect on your life, there are a few guidelines that are important to follow:

1. Do not eat for about an hour before or after practicing.
2. Do not practice too strenuously if you have a cold; also, beginners who tend to sweat a lot may be prone to catching a cold if there is a draft.
3. Do not start or finish abruptly; even after finishing slowly, do not undertake any vigorous activity right away, as it could cause headache and discomfort.
4. Do not practice immediately after taking a bath (the bath would be better after practice).
5. Try to relax completely before beginning to practice.
6. Try to calm the breath.
7. Practice regularly, and look for gradual improvement over time.

WARMING-UP QIGONG EXERCISES

(Dantian-gong dong-gong)

These exercises belong to a group of movements called *Qiangshen qigong* in Chinese, which means "body-strengthening exercises," although it might be more accurate to describe them as exercises that build up one's Qi. There are many different sets of these exercises practiced, but those given in this volume, the Warming-up Qigong exercises, or *Dantian-gong dong-gong* (literally, "moving exercises to fill the *dantian* with Qi"), consist of half a dozen relatively easy movements that beginners often learn before going on to more difficult types of exercises. Remember, however, that it is not the actual movement itself that is difficult, it is the correct performance of the movement in conjunction with proper regulation of the breath and the flow of Qi. Since they are so elementary, they have been included here as warming-up exercises that you might like to learn (or do) before moving on to the more difficult Everyday Stretching Qigong exercises that follow. These warming-up movements can be used for both external and internal forms. For internal forms, much greater emphasis and concentration should be placed upon controlling and directing the flow of Qi while performing them than is recommended here.

There are many forms of Qigong practice. Some are very quiet and are performed while seated; others are more active and seem more like exercises to Westerners. The Warming-up Qigong given here consists of a few simple postures that are each held for a short period of time. They are basically active exercises to help facilitate the free flow of Qi throughout the body, and also to build up your storehouse of Qi. Through practicing them, you can gather and store your own Qi and develop latent potential to your advantage. Because the Qi energy is made to flow more freely, these exercises often have the effect of relaxing tightened muscles, especially in the shoulders.

When performing this Warming-up Qigong set, you should perform each exercise 3–5 times (as recommended in the instructions below), gradually working up to as many as 50 repetitions. The successful performance of the exercises should take about 5 minutes at first, but if you are practicing only this set you should gradually

21 PREPARATION POSE

increase the number of repetitions so that it takes you anywhere from 15 to 45 minutes to do the set, which will help you to gain the greatest benefit. However, when you intend to do the Everyday Stretching Qigong exercises immediately after this set, a 5–10-minute set will suffice.

Preparation Pose *(Qi shi)*

Stand erect, with feet about shoulders' width apart. Hold your arms at your sides, but raise the hands slightly (Fig. 21). Relax and drop the shoulders and chest (rounding them), and look straight ahead; keep the mouth closed, with the teeth slightly touching and the tip of the tongue lightly touching the upper palate. Place your attention upon the *dantian,* or lower abdomen, and gently contract the anal sphincter.

1. Beginning Pose *(Yubei-shi)*
Bend both knees and place the hands on the thighs, bending the body forward like a bow; close the eyes, and concentrate on keeping the *dantian,* the body's energy storehouse, filled with Qi (Fig. 22).

Remaining in this position, practice abdominal breathing. Inhale slowly through the nose, letting the abdomen fill up with air. As you continue to inhale, feel the air filling up the lungs and stretching the

back like an expanding balloon. When you have taken a full breath, gently hold the breath for 7–8 seconds, or as long as is comfortable, remembering to keep the anal sphincter contracted. When ready, open the mouth and exhale slowly through it, letting the stomach pull back in naturally. After exhaling, stop breathing for another 7–8 seconds before resuming this exercise.

Repeat the process 3–5 times.

Note: In this posture, as in all the others, there should be a dual feeling of expanding/contracting, or rising/sinking such that when the breath (or the Qi) rises up you imagine, at the same time, a kind of sinking or pulling down. It is like a double movement of the breath/Qi both up to the head and down to the *dantian*, simultaneously. It is very important to retain this dual feeling in order for the exercises to be of maximum benefit.

2. Embrace Your Qi *(Pao dantian)*

Return to a standing position and assume the Preparation Pose. Even if indoors, feel yourself surrounded by nature. Calm your mind, dispel extraneous thoughts, and concentrate on the *dantian* being filled with Qi. Keep your eyes open, and look off into the distance as if gazing at the far horizon.

23	24

Take one step diagonally to the right with the right foot, and fall into a Right Bow Stance (your feet should be about 2 feet apart; the forward knee is bent and supports about 70% of the body's weight. When taking this position, let the back heel naturally shift its position). Next, while you raise both hands up to about eye level (leaving the elbows slightly bent and making the upper arms, which point out to the sides, almost parallel to the ground), slowly inhale through the nose, taking a very deep breath that completely fills first the lower abdomen and then the whole chest (Fig. 23). You will feel as though your body is expanding and straightening upward with the breath. Hold the breath for 7–8 seconds, or as long as is comfortable, and, as you slowly exhale through the mouth, drop both arms so that the hands come to rest in front of the *dantian*, or lower abdomen, as though embracing it with energy (Fig. 24). Stop breathing for another 7–8 seconds before slowly inhaling with the next repetition. Repeat 3–5 times on the right.

Now return to the Preparation Pose (*see* Fig. 21) and perform this exercise on the left. Take one step diagonally to the left with the left

25   26

foot, and fall into a Left Bow Stance. Next, while you raise both hands up to about eye level, slowly inhale, taking a very deep breath that completely fills first the lower abdomen and then the whole chest (Fig. 25). Hold the breath for 7–8 seconds, or as long as is comfortable. As you slowly exhale, drop both arms so that the hands come to rest in front of the *dantian,* or lower abdomen, as though embracing it with energy (Fig. 26). Stop breathing for another 7–8 seconds before inhaling with the next repetition. Repeat 3–5 times on the left.

3. Vertical Qi *(Shu dantian)*
Return to the Preparation Pose. While you slowly inhale through your nose, taking a full, deep breath, raise both arms up high. Separate the fingers and stretch as though reaching for the sky. (Make sure you keep the heels firmly planted on the ground.) While performing this, keep the eyes facing straight ahead (in other words, do not look up), and imagine that you are being pulled up like a

27   28

marionette by a string attached to the crown of your head. When fully
stretched, hold the posture and hold the breath for 3–5 seconds (Fig.
27). During all of this, imagine the Qi rising up in a straight line from
the contracted anal sphincter all the way up to the crown of the head
and then out into space.

Then, simultaneously, drop your arms into the position shown,
bend the knees to fall into a Small Horse-riding Stance, and harshly
and loudly expel all air through the mouth. The movements should
be quick and sudden, and while doing them, you should completely
relax your body (even the anal sphincter), and imagine Qi entering
through the crown of the head and filling up the *dantian* (Fig. 28).
Hold the breath for 3–5 seconds before doing the next repetition.

Repeat this exercise 3–5 times.

> **Benefits:** *This is a very purifying posture, which is thought to have a great
> beneficial effect upon the kidneys, the liver, the spleen, and the lungs. It
> is also said to help prevent colds.*

4. Pressing Down Your Qi *(Ya dantian)*
Return to the Preparation Pose. When you have relaxed and calmed
the mind, suddenly extend the knees and raise both arms up high so

| 29 | 30 |

that the palms face each other and the fingers point up to the sky. As you do this, inhale slowly but deeply, completely filling first the lower abdomen and then the chest, and inhaling through the nose. Keep the back as straight as possible, and bend the head so that you are looking up. Reach up high, and as you do, allow the heels to come up off the ground slightly (Fig. 29). While holding this position, allow the stretch on the abdomen to pull the lower abdomen in, and keep your anal sphincter contracted, imagining Qi rising from the toes to the hands and from the base of the spine up to the head. Hold your breath for about 3–5 seconds.

Then, as you slowly exhale through the mouth, lower the arms, keeping them bent with the hands placed in front of and to each side of the waist. As you do this, lower the heels back on the ground, bend the knees, and sink down into a squatting pose, making sure to keep the back perfectly straight and the head erect (Fig. 30). As you do this, imagine the Qi being pulled into your body and visualize it sinking down into the *dantian,* being pressed down by the hands. When all breath has been expelled, stop breathing for 3–5 seconds. Relax the whole body—including the anal sphincter—after you have done this.

Repeat 3–5 times.

31   32

Benefits: *This pose, like Posture 3, has long been thought to be extremely effective in purifying all the major organs of the body. It is often prescribed by Chinese doctors to help develop a body that cannot be harmed by disease* (buhuai zhi ti).

5. Casting Qi to the Side *(Heng [pie] dantian)*

Return to the Preparation Pose (Fig. 31). When you have relaxed and calmed the mind, take one step diagonally to the right, falling into a Right Bow Stance (as in Posture 2, p. 22). At the same time, raise the right arm, palm facing up, so it points up and to the right at a 45-degree angle away from the body, and raise the left arm, palm also facing up, so that your hand is held in front of the right armpit and your fingers point toward the right elbow (Fig. 32). Keep the eyes facing straight ahead (i.e., the eyes should look straight ahead in the direction in which the body faces, not at the right hand). Although the right hand is held high, be careful not to raise the right shoulder. While assuming this pose, slowly inhale deeply and completely through the nose. Hold the pose, and hold your breath, for 3–5 seconds. Keep the anal sphincter contracted, and be careful to keep the back perfectly straight. Imagine the Qi rising up from the *dantian,* which stays sunken, and traveling up to the hands. As you slowly exhale through the mouth, return to the Preparation Pose.

33

34

When you have relaxed and calmed your mind, take one step diagonally to the left, falling into a Left Bow Stance (as in Posture 2, p. 23). At the same time, raise the left arm, palm facing up, to point up and to the left at a 45-degree angle away from the body. Raise the right arm, palm also facing up, so that your hand is held before the left armpit and your fingers point toward the left elbow (Fig. 33). Keep the eyes facing straight ahead (i.e., the eyes should look straight ahead in the direction in which your body faces, not at the left hand). Although the left hand is held high, be careful not to raise the left shoulder. While assuming this pose, slowly inhale deeply and completely through the nose. Hold the pose, and hold your breath, for 3–5 seconds. Keep the anal sphincter contracted, and be careful to keep the back perfectly straight. Imagine the Qi rising up from the *dantian,* which stays sunken, and traveling up to your hands. As you slowly exhale through the mouth, return to the Preparation Pose.

6. Gathering Qi *(Shou gong)*
Now that you have performed the basic movements of Warming-up Qigong, your Qi should be flowing in a harmonious manner, and the reserves of Qi in your *dantian* should be replete.

Now return to the position described in Posture 1 (Fig. 34). Inhale slowly through the nose 3–5 times, as instructed in Posture 1. With each inhalation, press the teeth together firmly; this should produce a quantity of saliva. Do not swallow it between breaths; keep it in the mouth. After taking the last breath, and while holding the breath, mix it around in the mouth 3 times and then swallow it, imagining that it is cleansing the whole body and infusing it with life force. The ancient Taoist sages referred to this liquid as "the elixir of immortality," and considered it essential for anyone who wanted to live a long and healthy life. After swallowing the "elixir of immortality," slowly exhale, and feel all the energy surrounding you enter your body and sink down into the *dantian*. Then slowly return to the Preparation Pose and relax for a few seconds, allowing your Qi to sink even further. Take 3–5 slow but deep breaths, and then you have finished and may go on to live an energy-filled day or proceed to the Everyday Qigong Exercises for even more health-enhancing exercise.

EVERYDAY STRETCHING QIGONG

(Yijinjing)

These exercises are among the best known in China, and are so old that they are said to have been passed down to later generations from the *Classic of Muscular Development (Yijinjing)* written by Bodhidharma, the Indian monk who brought Zen to China in about A.D. 526 and is revered as the father of the Shaolin school of martial arts. When Bodhidharma arrived at the Shaolin Temple—which had been founded on the peak of Mt. Song in Henan province in either 377 or 496, he discovered that the monks were in a deplorable state of physical unfitness. Thus, he developed a series of exercises by which the monks could strengthen their bodies—not only to help them withstand the rigors of long hours of meditation, but also to give them a means of defending themselves against mountain brigands. This set of exercises is called *Yijinjing* in Chinese, which can mean "exercises (*yi*) to stretch/develop (*jing*) the muscles (*jin*)." Thought to be based upon the everyday movements of farmers working in the fields, and practiced by the Chinese for centuries, the movements make up an exercise routine that both relaxes and strengthens the muscles and tendons. Great emphasis is placed upon breathing abdominally in these exercises, which makes them ideal for beginners. They are even good for those who cannot yet breathe comfortably with the abdomen, since they comprise a wonderful training program for abdominal breathing.

Here we have divided them into three sections, the first and last of which have 10 exercises, and the second, 12. The postures given are simplified versions that have come from the ancient past. Although each can be thought of, and performed, as a separate exercise, there is more benefit derived from doing them in sequence.

When performing the exercises, you should at first try to do them while practicing abdominal breathing (letting the lower stomach push out during inhalation and pull in during exhalation, while the chest remains relatively still). You should not forcefully push the stomach out or strain to pull it in, but rather let it learn to do so naturally. Eventually, deep abdominal breathing will become second nature to you. Those more advanced might like to experiment with reverse breathing (with the abdomen held in during inhalation and allowed to expand during exhalation, again with the chest remaining relatively still); this is a Taoist technique that helps one to build up Qi, but it is more effective if one has mastered the other technique first. Each of these methods of breathing is beneficial in terms of the massage and strength it gives to the internal organs, but most people will benefit the most by just learning to breathe naturally with the abdomen, which will allow the Qi to flow more smoothly. You should refrain from reverse breathing until you have worked up the number of repetitions you perform to about 30 or 40. When doing the exercises, remember to take a few deep breaths before you start to help you relax and to settle the breath. Whichever breath-manipulating technique you choose, remember to breathe deeply and to inhale slowly and then retain the air while using the diaphragm to push the stomach out. Exhalation should also be slow and even, as any irregularity in the breath or anxiety the method of breathing may cause will upset the flow of Qi.

SECTION 1

Section 1 consists of a few simple breathing exercises. Those just starting to do the exercises should repeat each of the 10 postures only 3 to 5 times, and, as mentioned in the instructions below, gradually work up to about 10. Those who have been doing the exercises for a while can *gradually* increase the number up to about 40 or 50.

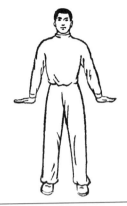

Preparation Pose *(Qi shi)*

Stand erect, with feet about shoulders' width apart. Clench the fists, but point the thumbs toward the thighs (Fig. 35). Relax, drop the shoulders and chest (rounding them), and look straight ahead. Keep the mouth closed, with the teeth slightly touching and the tip of the tongue lightly touching the upper palate. Place your attention upon the *dantian,* or lower abdomen, and gently contract the anal sphincter.

1. Clenched-Fist Breathing *(Woquan huxi)*

Standing in the position described above; inhale slowly, pushing out the lower abdomen and relaxing your fists. Then exhale slowly, pulling the lower abdomen in and tightening the fists. Repeat 3–5 times.

2. Pressing-Down Breathing *(Anzhang huxi)*

Standing in the same position, bend the hands up, so that the palms seem to press down as your fingers point outward (Fig. 36).

Inhale slowly, pushing the lower abdomen out and holding your hands in the position described above. Be careful not to bend your legs.

Then exhale slowly, pulling the lower abdomen in and stretching the arms while pressing down. When exhaling, bend the fingers up as

30 • CHAPTER 1

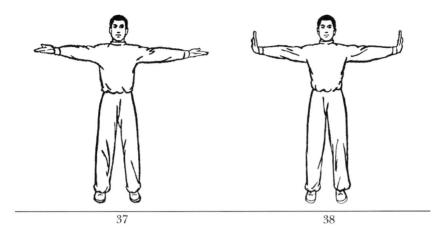

37   38

far as possible, tensing the arms, shoulders, and whole body as much as you can. Repeat 3–5 times.

3. Palms-Up Breathing *(Tuozhang huxi)*
Standing in the same position, stretch the arms out and bring them up to shoulder level, with the palms facing up (Fig. 37).

Inhale slowly, pushing the lower abdomen out and holding your arms in the position described above. Be careful not to bend your legs.

Then exhale slowly, pulling the lower abdomen in and stretching the arms out to the sides as much as possible. Repeat 3–5 times.

4. Palms-Out Breathing *(Chengzhang huxi)*
Standing in the same position, keep your arms at shoulder level and bend your wrists so that the palms are facing out and the fingers are pointing up (Fig. 38).

Inhale slowly, pushing the lower abdomen out and holding your arms in the position described above. Be careful not to bend your legs.

Then exhale slowly, pulling the lower abdomen in and pushing your open palms out to the sides. When exhaling, try to bend the fingers backward as much as possible, so they point toward your head. Repeat 3–5 times.

39	40

5. Praying-Palm Breathing *(Kaihe huxi)*

Standing in the same position, lower your arms and hold your palms together in front of you so that the fingers are pointing up and the thumbs are touching the chest (Fig. 39).

Inhale slowly, pushing your lower abdomen out and holding your arms in the position described above. Be careful not to bend your legs. As you inhale, slowly move your palms out to your sides, with the thumbs sliding across the chest (Fig. 40).

Exhale slowly, pulling the lower abdomen in, and slowly push your open palms back together into the prayer position. When they come together, continue to press them as much as possible, as though performing an isometric exercise, until the breath is completely expelled. Repeat 3–5 times.

6. Pushing-Up, Hanging-Down Breathing *(Shangcheng xiachui huxi)*

Step off to the left, bending the left knee and keeping the right leg straight. Place 70% of your weight on the front leg. Raise your left arm and hold your hand with the palm facing up (the thumb should be on the front side of the palm). Lower your right hand so that the palm faces the thigh and points down toward the ground (Fig. 41).

32 • CHAPTER 1

41   42

Inhale slowly, pushing the lower abdomen out and holding your arms in the position described above. Be careful not to bend your legs. As you inhale, slowly push the left palm up and the right hand down, tensing the whole body as much as possible as you breathe in. Then relax as you exhale slowly, pulling the lower abdomen in. Repeat 3–5 times.

Now step off to the right, bending the right knee and keeping the left leg straight. Keep the upper body erect; do not lean forward. Raise the right arm and hold your hand with the palm facing up (the thumb should be on the front side of the palm). Lower the left hand so that the palm faces the thigh and points down toward the ground (Fig. 42).

Inhale slowly, pushing the lower abdomen out and holding your arms in the position described above. Be careful not to bend your legs. As you inhale, slowly push the right palm up and the left hand down, tensing the whole body as much as possible as you breathe in. Then relax as you exhale slowly, pulling the lower abdomen in.

This represents one repetition. Repeat 3–5 times. You may either do your complete number of repetitions on each side, or alternate left, right, left, right, until you finish.

43   44

7. Knee-Bend Breathing *(Qifu huxi)*

Come back to the original position, but this time stand so that your feet are just a little further than shoulders' width apart. Be careful to keep the upper body erect throughout the knee bend.

Stretch your arms straight out in front of you, each hand directly in front of its shoulder, palm up (Fig. 43).

Inhale slowly, pushing the lower abdomen out and holding your arms in the position described above. Then exhale slowly, pulling in the lower abdomen. While exhaling, turn your palms over so that they face down, and bend the knees until your thighs are parallel to the ground (Fig. 44).

Then inhale slowly, pushing the lower abdomen out. While inhaling, turn the palms over so that they face up (Fig. 45). At the same time, slowly extend the legs so that you return to the standing posture. (Fig. 46)

This represents one repetition. Repeat 3–5 times.

> ***Benefits:*** *When performed regularly, this exercise energizes the whole body, particularly the kidneys and the lower back.*

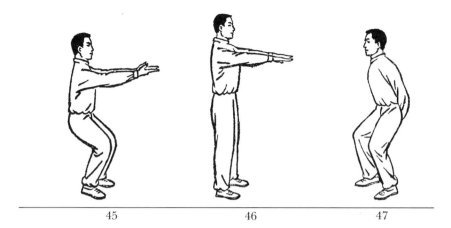

45   46   47

8. Half-Squat Breathing *(Zhanzhuang huxi)*
Standing in the same position, bend both knees and assume a half-squatting position. Hold your hands behind your back, grasping the right fist with the left hand (Fig. 47). Try to stand as erect as possible, realizing that natural posture is a slightly forward-bending one, as seen in the figure.

Inhale slowly, pushing the lower abdomen out and holding the arms in the position described above; be careful not to bend your legs any further. As you inhale, try to push the abdomen out as far as possible without straining.

Then exhale slowly, gently pulling in the lower abdomen as far as possible without straining.

This represents one repetition. Repeat 3–5 times.

Benefits: *When performed regularly, this exercise helps to lower the blood pressure; it also strengthens the leg muscles and builds up stamina.*

48   49

9. Forward-Bend Breathing *(Xiafu huxi)*

Return to an upright position, and place the feet shoulders' width apart, with your arms hanging loose at your sides, palms facing in, and fingers pointing to the ground (Fig. 48).

Inhale slowly, pushing the lower abdomen out and holding your arms in the position described above. Be careful not to bend your legs any further.

Then exhale slowly, pulling in the lower abdomen. While exhaling, bend the upper body forward until it is parallel with the ground, let the arms hang freely, and relax the shoulders (Fig. 49). Those who are supple enough can touch the ground, but no one should ever strain to do so.

Then inhale slowly, pushing out the lower abdomen. While inhaling, slowly straighten the body and return to the upright position.

This represents one repetition. Repeat 3–5 times.

> *Benefits: When performed regularly, this exercise helps to decrease the amount of fat accumulated in the abdomen; it also helps to alleviate lower-back pain.*

10. Back-Twist Breathing *(Aoshen-huiwang huxi)*

Step off to the left, bending the left knee and keeping the right leg straight. Place 70% of your weight on the front leg. Twist your body

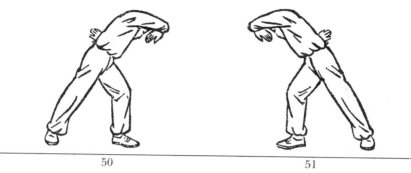

50   51

to the left, placing the left hand upon the small of the back, palm facing out and thumb pointing up. Bend the right arm and hold the right hand directly in front of the forehead, palm facing out and thumb pointing down (Fig. 50). Look at the right heel, which should remain planted firmly upon the ground.

Inhale slowly, pushing your lower abdomen out and holding your arms in the position described above. Be careful not to bend your legs further. As you inhale, tense the whole body as much as possible, and try to twist even more to the left. Then relax as you exhale slowly, pulling the lower abdomen in. While exhaling, imagine that you are lowering your weight to the right heel.

Step off to the right, bending the right knee and keeping the left leg straight. Your weight should be about 70% on the front leg. Twist your body to the right, placing the right hand upon the small of the back, the palm facing out and the thumb pointing up. Bend the left arm and hold the left hand directly in front of the forehead, the palm facing out and the thumb pointing down. (Fig. 51). Look at the left heel, which should remain planted firmly upon the ground.

Inhale slowly, pushing the lower abdomen out and holding your arms in the position described above. Be careful not to bend your legs further. As you inhale, tense the whole body as much as possible, and try to twist even more to the right. Then relax as you exhale slowly, pulling the lower abdomen in. While exhaling, imagine that you are lowering your weight to your left heel.

This represents one repetition. Repeat 3–5 times.

Benefits: When performed regularly, this exercise helps to alleviate back and shoulder pain; it also gives more suppleness to the waist and massages the inner organs.

This completes Section 1, which is basically a set of warming-up exercises. If you wish to stop exercising here, simply return to the upright position, take a few deep breaths, relax, and breathe naturally for a few seconds; then you can go about your business. If you wish to continue, simply return to the upright position and proceed as described below, altering the upright position slightly to match the preparation pose described below.

SECTION 2

Section 2 consists of 12 movements based upon the daily work of grain farmers in their fields. This set of exercises is especially good for toning up and strengthening debilitated or weakened muscles.

Preparation Position *(Qi shi)*
Stand erect, with feet about shoulders' width apart. Hold your arms by your sides, resting the palms upon the thighs (Fig. 52). Relax, drop the shoulders and chest (rounding them), and look straight ahead; keep the mouth closed, with the teeth slightly touching, and the tip of the tongue lightly touching the upper palate. Place your attention upon the *dantian*, or lower abdomen, and gently contract the anal sphincter.

11. Pounding and Husking Grain *(Daochu chongliang)*
Standing in the position described above, place your hands in front of your chest so that the elbows point out to the sides and the palms face each other, about 10 cm (about 4 in) apart, with the fingers pointing up (Fig. 53).

Bring the palms together into a praying position and inhale slowly, pushing the lower abdomen out. Be careful not to bend your legs. While inhaling, keep the entire palms of both hands touching, but try to bend the fingers backward and outward.

Then exhale slowly, pulling in the lower abdomen. While exhaling, relax the hands and forearms. (This will cause the fingers to relax naturally.) Repeat 3–5 times.

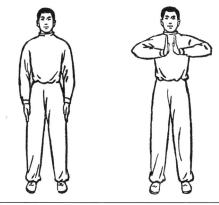

52 PREPARATION POSE   53

54

12. Shouldering Grain with a Pole *(Biandan tiaoliang)*

Standing in the same position, stretch the arms slowly out to the sides, and open the palms, facing outward, so that the fingers point up (Fig. 54).

Inhale slowly, pushing the lower abdomen out. Be careful not to bend your legs. While inhaling, throw out and expand your chest by gently pushing your extended arms to the back as far as possible, and keep the fingers pointing straight up.

Then exhale slowly, pulling in the lower abdomen. While exhaling, deflate the chest and bring your arms back to your sides while bending the fingers backward and pushing the base of the palms out. Repeat 3–5 times.

55   56

13. Separating the Chaff from the Grain *(Yangfeng jingliang)*

Standing in the same position, raise both arms above your head, and extend them so that the elbows are straight, the palms point up, and the fingers point toward each other. Extend and stretch the entire body upward (Fig. 55).

Inhale slowly, pushing the lower abdomen out. Be careful not to bend your legs. While inhaling, take the air in through your nose, and try to push your palms up as far as possible.

Then exhale slowly, pulling in the lower abdomen. While exhaling, expel the air through your mouth, and relax the whole body (while remaining erect). Repeat 3–5 times.

14. Carrying a Sack of Grain on Your Shoulders *(Huanjian kangliang)*

Standing in the Preparation Position, raise only your right arm above your head, and hold it so that your palm faces down (Fig. 56). Look at your palm, and put your left hand on the small of your back, palm facing out.

Inhale slowly, pushing the lower abdomen out. Be careful not to bend your legs. While inhaling, stretch your head up and pull the shoulders back as far as possible.

57   58

Then exhale slowly, pulling in the lower abdomen. While exhaling, relax the whole body (while remaining erect).

Now, still standing in the same position, raise only the left arm above the head, and hold it so that the palm faces down (Fig. 57). Place your eyes on your palm, and put the right hand on the small of the back, palm facing out.

Inhale slowly, pushing the lower abdomen out. Be careful not to bend your legs. While inhaling, stretch your head up and pull your shoulders back as far as possible.

Then exhale slowly, pulling in the lower abdomen. While exhaling, relax the whole body (while remaining erect).

This represents one repetition. Repeat 3–5 times. You may either do your complete number of repetitions on each side, or alternate left, right, left, right, until you finish. Also, while you perform this exercise, your body might tend to turn to one side or the other. As much as possible, try to keep your toes pointing straight ahead.

15. Stacking Sacks of Grain *(Tuidai duoliang)*
Standing in the same position, stretch both of your arms straight out in front of you, each arm directly in front of its shoulder, but then point the fingers up so that the palms face out (Fig. 58). You should look straight ahead.

Inhale slowly, pushing the lower abdomen out. Be careful not to bend your legs. While inhaling, try to push your palms out as far as possible, and bend the fingers backward.

Then exhale slowly, pulling in the lower abdomen. While exhaling, relax the whole body (remaining erect), letting your fingers return to the upward-pointing position. Repeat 3–5 times.

16. Pulling an Ox Laden with Grain (*Qianniu laliang*)

Drop your arms and stand in the Preparation Position (*see* Fig. 52). Turn 90 degrees to the right and take a step with the right leg, bending the right knee and keeping the left knee straight. Raise the right fist, palm facing out, above your head; your arms should be held pointing straight ahead and directly in front of the right shoulder, the elbow bent about 120 degrees. The left fist, palm facing out, should be held near the small of the back on the left side (Fig. 59).

Inhale slowly, pushing the lower abdomen out. Be careful not to bend your legs further. While inhaling, clench the fists as tightly as possible and bend them in toward the body.

Then exhale slowly, pulling in the lower abdomen. While exhaling, relax the whole body (remaining erect), letting the fists return to their original position.

Then drop the arms and stand in the Preparation Position. Turn 90 degrees to the left and take a step with the left leg, bending the left knee and keeping the right knee straight. Raise the left fist, palm facing out, above your head. The arm should be held pointing straight ahead and held directly in front of the left shoulder, the elbow bent about 120 degrees. The right fist, palm facing out, should be held at the small of the back on the right side (Fig 60).

Inhale slowly, pushing the lower abdomen out. Be careful not to bend your leg further. While inhaling, clench the fists as tightly as possible and bend them in toward the body.

Then exhale slowly, pulling in the lower abdomen. While exhaling, relax the whole body (while remaining erect), letting the fists return to their original position.

This represents one repetition. Repeat 3–5 times. You may either do the complete number of repetitions on each side, or alternate left, right, left, right, until you finish.

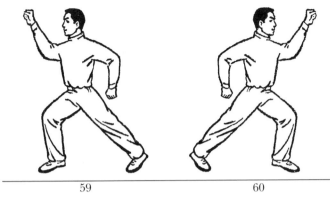

59   60

61

17. Carrying Grain on Your Back *(Beiqian yunliang)*

Return to the Preparation Position, and place your left hand on your mid-back, palm facing out and fingers reaching up; then place your right hand on your upper back, palm facing in and fingers reaching down. Grasp the fingers of the left hand with your right hand (Fig. 61).

Inhale slowly, pushing the lower abdomen out. Be careful not to bend your legs. While inhaling, pull the fingers of your left hand upward.

62

Then exhale slowly, pulling in the lower abdomen. While exhaling, relax the whole body (while remaining erect), letting the fingers fall to their original position.

Then return to the Preparation Position, and place your right hand on your mid-back, palm facing out and fingers reaching up. Place your left hand on your upper back, palm facing in and fingers reaching down. Grasp the fingers of the right hand with your left hand (Fig. 62).

Inhale slowly, pushing the lower abdomen out. Be careful not to bend your legs. While inhaling, pull the fingers of your right hand upward.

Then exhale slowly, pulling in the lower abdomen. While exhaling, relax the whole body (while remaining erect), letting the fingers drop to their original position.

This represents one repetition. Repeat 3–5 times. You may either do your complete number of repetitions on each side, or alternate left, right, left, right, until you finish.

Benefits: *This exercise will strengthen the muscles, improve circulation, and relieve tension in the chest, back, and shoulders.*

63   64

18. Unloading Baskets of Grain *(Panluo xieliang)*
Take a step sideways to the left so that the feet are about shoulders' width-and-a-half apart. Bend your knees and fall into a Horse-riding Stance. Keep the upper body erect, and hold the arms out to the sides so the elbows are bent, the palms face up as though supporting a heavy load, and the lower arms are parallel to the ground (Fig. 63).

Remain in this position for a while, then inhale slowly, pushing the lower abdomen out. Be careful not to bend your legs further. While inhaling, imagine the load getting heavier.

Then exhale slowly, pulling in the lower abdomen. While exhaling, relax the whole body (while remaining erect), and, turning the palms face down (Fig. 64), slowly rise up into a standing position in which the legs are straight and the feet are together.

Then inhale slowly, pushing the lower abdomen out. While inhaling, turn the palms face up, slowly bend the knees, and fall into the Horse-riding Stance described above.

One rising and falling represents one repetition. Repeat 3–5 times.

Benefits: *This exercise will strengthen the muscles in the legs, lower abdomen, and lower back.*

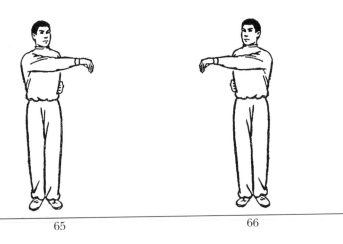

65   66

19. Wrapping Straw Mats Around the Grain (Weibao tunliang)

Return to the Preparation Position. Clench the left fist and hold it at the waist, then reach out across the body to the left with the right hand, arm parallel to the ground and fingers curled and facing down, as though grasping a straw mat (Fig. 65).

Inhale slowly, pushing the lower abdomen out. While inhaling, keep the body erect.

Then exhale slowly, pulling in the lower abdomen. While exhaling, relax the whole body, twist the upper body to the left and bend forward, then twist back to the right (to face forward) and straighten up to the original position, making certain to adjust the position of the right arm to match that shown in Figure 65. Also, when twisting the waist, move the hands in a circular motion, as though wrapping a straw mat around the grain.

This represents one repetition. Repeat 3–5 times, and then perform on the other side.

Return to the Preparation Position. Clench the right fist and hold it at the waist, then reach out across the body to the right with the left hand, arm parallel to the ground and fingers curled and facing down, as though grasping a straw mat (Fig. 66).

Inhale slowly, pushing the lower abdomen out. While inhaling, keep the body erect.

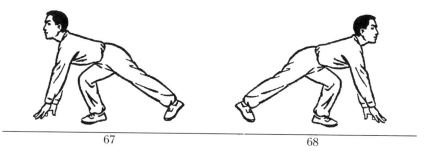

67   68

Then exhale slowly, pulling in the lower abdomen. While exhaling, relax the whole body, twist the upper body to the right and bend forward, then twist back to the left (to face forward) and straighten up to the original position, making certain to adjust the position of the left arm to match that shown in Figure 66. Also, when twisting the waist, move the hands in a circular motion, as though wrapping a straw mat around the grain.

This represents one repetition. Repeat 3–5 times.

20. Catching Locusts *(Pudi huliang)*

Return to the Preparation Position. Take one step with the right leg. Keeping the left leg straight, bend the right knee, and lower the upper body so that you touch the ground with both hands. Try to keep the back straight and the head erect (Fig. 67). The movements described below are based on the action of a farmer searching for and catching locusts and other grain-eating pests.

Inhale slowly, pushing the lower abdomen out. While inhaling, straighten the arms and lift the chest up. Be careful not to bend or extend the legs.

Then exhale slowly, pulling in the lower abdomen. While exhaling, bend the arms and lower the chest. Be careful not to bend or extend the legs.

This represents one repetition. Repeat 3–5 times, then change sides.

Return to the Preparation Position. Take one step with the left leg. Keeping the right leg straight, bend the left knee and lower the upper body so that you touch the ground with both hands. Try to keep the back straight and the head erect (Fig. 68).

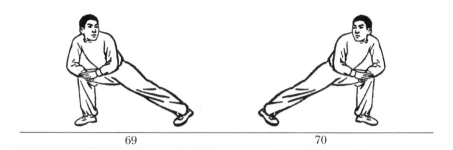

Inhale slowly, pushing the lower abdomen out. While inhaling, straighten the arms and lift the chest up. Be careful not to bend or extend the legs.

Then exhale slowly, pulling in the lower abdomen. While exhaling, bend the arms and lower the chest. Be careful not to bend or extend the legs.

This represents one repetition. Repeat 3–5 times.

Alternative Pose: If the pose described above is too difficult for you, you can perform it by resting your hands upon your bent knee (Figs. 69, 70), instead of placing them on the ground.

> **Benefits:** *This exercise not only increases your overall strength but also improves your sense of balance. When done properly, it is very good for the lower back and shoulders.*

21. Gathering the Grain *(Quti jianliang)*
Return to the Preparation Position. Place the hands on top of the head, the fingers almost touching on the crown of the head, and tap the head lightly with the fingers for a few minutes.

Then exhale slowly, pulling in the lower abdomen. While exhaling, put the head between the bent knees and slowly expel all the air remaining in your lungs (Fig. 71).

71   72

Then inhale slowly, pushing out the lower abdomen. While inhaling, slowly come back up to a standing position. Remain erect, tapping the head with the fingers, until the lungs are completely full. *This represents one repetition.* Repeat 3–5 times.

> **Benefits:** *This exercise will strengthen the muscles in the back; tapping the head is said to stimulate the brain and rejuvenate the memory; it is also thought to be beneficial in invigorating the scalp and in slowing down the thinning of the hair.*

22. Scooping Up the Grain *(Gongshen shouliang)*
Return to the Preparation Position. Exhale slowly, pulling the lower abdomen in. While exhaling, bend forward, keeping the knees straight, but allowing the heels to rise up off the ground; let the arms hang loose, but hold the palms up, fingers facing inward. Keep your head raised, facing forward, and try to touch the ground with the back of your hands (Fig. 72).

Then inhale slowly, pushing out the lower abdomen. While inhaling, come back into the Preparation Position, letting the heels fall back to the ground.
This represents one repetition. Repeat 3–5 times.

73

After finishing the repetitions, and while still standing in the Preparation Position, spread the arms out to the sides, keeping the elbows bent and the palms facing inward (Fig. 73). Stretch the arms out to the sides and bend them back in seven times.

This completes Section 2, which is basically a set of exercises to limber up the body and keep the waist and lower back flexible while making the legs strong. If you wish to stop exercising here, simply return to the upright position, take a few deep breaths, relax, and breathe naturally for a few seconds; then you can go about your business. If you wish to continue, simply return to the upright position and proceed as described below, altering the upright position slightly to match the poses described below.

SECTION 3

Section 3 consists of 10 movements that are essentially cooling-down exercises. In addition to utilizing the breathing, they also use inner force and place great emphasis upon concentration. Thus, although they appear to be very simple exercises to perform, it is very difficult to do them properly. At first, if it is easier for you, you may forget about the breathing and just concentrate on performing the movements, adding the breathing later. Each movement may be performed up to 50 times, depending upon your physical condition,

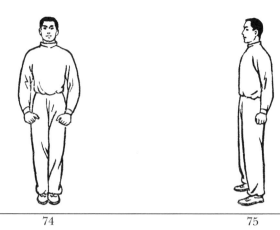

74   75

but we recommend that you start with 3–5 repetitions and slowly increase the number.

23. Lifting Your Thumbs *(Qiaomuzhi)*
Stand at attention. Clench each hand into a fist, but let the thumbs point out toward each other, and rest your fists on your thighs.

Inhale slowly, pushing the lower abdomen out; be careful not to bend your legs. While inhaling, tighten your fists and tense the whole body as much as possible, then try to lift your thumbs upward with inner force (Fig. 74).

Then exhale slowly, pulling in the lower abdomen. While exhaling, relax the whole body (while remaining erect), letting the thumbs return to the horizontal pointing position. Repeat 3–5 times.

24. Holding Your Thumbs *(Wogu)*
Stand with feet shoulders' width apart and let the arms hang loose by your sides. Bend the thumbs and clench the fingers over them, making fists.

Inhale slowly, pushing the lower abdomen out; be careful not to bend your legs. While inhaling, try to tighten your fists as much as possible, using inner force (Fig. 75).

Then exhale slowly, pulling in the lower abdomen. While exhaling, relax the whole body (remaining erect), loosening the fists. Repeat 3–5 times.

76   77

25. Holding Your Arms Forward (*Qianping-ju*)

Stand at attention. Form fists over your thumbs.

Inhale slowly, pushing the lower abdomen out; be careful not to bend your legs. While inhaling, slowly raise your arms out to the front and slightly inward, and bring them up to shoulder level, keeping the elbows bent, and holding the fists, which should face each other, about 30 cm (12 in) apart. When raising the fists, use inner force to tighten the fists and tense the whole body as much as possible (Fig. 76).

Then exhale slowly, pulling in the lower abdomen. While exhaling, relax the whole body (remaining erect), slowly lowering your fists back to your sides. Repeat 3–5 times.

26. Raising Your Arms Overhead (*Shang-ju*)

Stand at attention. Form fists over your thumbs.

Inhale slowly, pushing the lower abdomen out; be careful not to bend your legs. While inhaling, slowly raise your arms out to the front, and bring them up overhead as high as they will go, keeping the elbows bent and holding the fists, which should face each other, about 50 cm (18 in) apart. When raising the fists, use inner force to tighten them, tensing the whole body as much as possible, and lift the heels off the ground (Fig. 77).

Then exhale slowly, pulling in the lower abdomen. While exhal-

78   79

ing, relax the whole body (remaining erect), slowly lowering your heels and bringing your fists back to your sides. Repeat 3–5 times.

27. Holding Your Fists by Your Ears *(Er-quan)*

Stand with your feet shoulders' width apart, toes facing outward about 45 degrees. Form fists over your thumbs.

Inhale slowly, pushing the lower abdomen out; be careful not to bend your legs. While inhaling, slowly raise your arms out to the sides and bend the elbows so that the fists are held near the ears, palms facing out. When raising the fists, use inner force to tighten the fists and tense the whole body as much as possible (Fig. 78).

Then exhale slowly, pulling in the lower abdomen. While exhaling, relax the whole body (while remaining erect), slowly lowering your fists back to your sides. Repeat 3–5 times.

28. Lifting Your Toes *(Qiaozhi)*

Stand at attention, but let the toes face out. Form fists over your thumbs, and raise your arms out to the sides, so that your body forms a cross and the fists face forward.

Inhale slowly, pushing the lower abdomen out; be careful not to bend your legs. While inhaling, lift your toes off the ground, slowly press your arms back toward the rear, and lean backward slightly. In this position, use inner force to tighten the fists and tense the whole body as much as possible (Fig. 79).

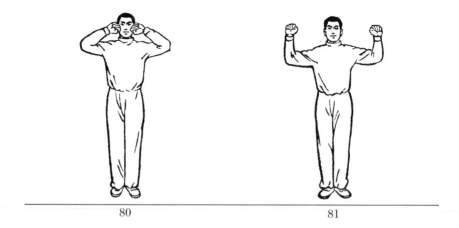

80   81

Then exhale slowly, pulling in the lower abdomen. While exhaling, relax the whole body (while remaining erect), slowly lowering your heels and dropping your fists back to your sides. Repeat 3–5 times.

29. Holding Fists Near Your Nose *(Bi-quan)*
Stand at attention, but let the toes face out. Form fists over your thumbs, raise your arms out to the sides, and then bend your elbows so that your fists, which face forward, are held about 5 cm (2 in) from either side of your nose. The upper arms should be almost parallel to the ground (Fig. 80).

Inhale slowly, pushing the lower abdomen out; be careful not to bend your legs. While inhaling, use inner force to tighten the fists and tense the whole body as much as possible.

Then exhale slowly, pulling in the lower abdomen. While exhaling, relax the whole body (while remaining erect). Repeat 3–5 times.

30. Holding Fists High *(Shan-quan)*
Stand at attention, but let the toes face out. Form fists over your thumbs, raise your arms out to the sides, and then bend your elbows so that your fists, which face forward, are held upright on either side of your head. The upper arm should be almost parallel to the ground, while the lower arm points straight up (Fig. 81).

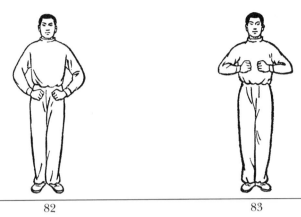

82   83

Inhale slowly, pushing the lower abdomen out; be careful not to bend your legs. While inhaling, use inner force to tighten the fists and tense the whole body as much as possible.

Then exhale slowly, pulling in the lower abdomen. While exhaling, relax the whole body (while remaining erect). Repeat 3–5 times.

31. Holding Fists Near Your Navel *(Qi-quan)*
Stand at attention, but let the toes face out. Form fists over your thumbs, and then bend your elbows so that your fists, which face downward, are held on either side of your navel (Fig. 82).

Inhale slowly, pushing the lower abdomen out; be careful not to bend your legs. While inhaling, use inner force to tighten the fists and tense the whole body as much as possible.

Then exhale slowly, pulling in the lower abdomen. While exhaling, relax the whole body (while remaining erect). Repeat 3–5 times.

32. Holding Fists at Your Chest *(Xiong-quan)*
Stand at attention, but let the toes face out. Form fists over your thumbs, raise your arms out to the sides, and then bend your elbows so that your fists, which face downward, are held directly in front of each breast. The upper arms should be almost parallel to the ground (Fig. 83).

Inhale slowly, pushing the lower abdomen out; be careful not to bend your legs. While inhaling, use inner force to tighten the fists and tense the whole body as much as possible.

Then exhale slowly, pulling in the lower abdomen. While exhaling, relax the whole body (while remaining erect). Repeat 3–5 times.

Finishing

To finish the Everyday Stretching Qigong exercises, whether at the end of the first, second, or third section, stand erect, with your feet about shoulders' width apart, as in the Preparation Position, but extend the fingers—that is, do not clench the hands into fists.

First, inhale slowly and deeply, through your nose, completely filling the lungs, first expanding the lower abdomen and then letting the breath fill up the entire space within the lungs. As you inhale, you should rotate your arms, which remain straight, so that the palms turn over to face forward and the arms slide a little out to the side and back.

Then, as you exhale slowly through the mouth, let the arms fall back into their natural position by your sides, and relax the whole body. Repeat 3–5 times.

2

Internal Forms (Nei-gong)

PRINCIPLES

Many systems of exercise have been developed throughout history, all over the world, and all of them are good for the health—if done properly. But most of them were devised to strengthen the physical body and give one greater power and a more fear-inspiring physique.

The traditional Chinese exercises given here, however, were especially formulated to help prevent certain diseases. They were also performed to build up one's reserves of Qi, to strengthen the body from the inside out, and to make one invulnerable to common ailments. (Indeed, martial-arts experts even tried to make their bodies impervious to any form of injury they might sustain in an attack through their rigorous use of numerous Qigong techniques far too complicated to go into here. Whether or not they succeeded in their task is not known; it is certain, however, that many of the adherents of such practices were killed by Western bullets in the Boxer Uprising of 1898–1900.) Although most of the Chinese sets of Qigong exercises have been simplified and revised by modern experts, they are still thought to be extremely beneficial to health.

The effects that these exercises have upon the body have given rise to the names by which we know them today. The set given here as the Life-Prolonging Qigong *(Qubing-yannian ershi-shi)* is more properly classified as an external form of Qigong, and is very similar to the Everyday Stretching Qigong; but as the movements are described in ancient Chinese texts as having a beneficial effect on joint disorders and various systemic problems within the body, we have decided to include them here. The version given here is the revised set that was refined and taught by Dr. Wang Ziping (1881–1973), a native of Hebei province (and a student of numerous forms of martial arts and Qigong, as well as a doctor trained in both traditional and Western medicine). Dr. Wang's revised Life-Prolonging Qigong set is based upon the ancient Five Animal Forms *(Wuqinxi)* and contains 20 movements that affect all parts of the body—every muscle, ligament, and joint. The number and variety of movements is great, and the instructions are divided into two sections—Preparation and Movement—in order to make each of the 20 movements easier to learn.

When performing these and any other Qigong exercises, it is important to perform them slowly and rhythmically. Some even find that it helps to count out the beats (like in dancing or marching) as they do the set. It is also important to follow the illustrations as closely as possible and to perform the different poses and movements as accurately as you can. Remember that the greatest benefit will be obtained by stretching all parts of the body as much as possible, and that breathing should be done in conjunction with the movements.

The other set given here, the 13 Grand Preservers Qigong set *(Shisan taibao-gong),* is based upon an ancient system of Taoist breathing exercises that has been joined with Qigong exercises developed through the various internal martial arts (that is, those self-defense systems that do not rely upon muscular strength but depend upon the ability of the student to produce and effectively use his own inner force, or Qi). It has come down to us from olden times as an excellent method of preserving youthful vigor and health.

The method of teaching this form of Qigong was always a secret one that involved direct oral transmission of the art—along with physical instruction from a teacher to a student, and thus, for many centuries, even the existence of this great system of health maintenance was not known. However, the famous Dr. Wang Ziping passed on the secret teachings of the form to a few people, starting in about 1965. Since that time, it has spread and gained great popularity in the Chinese-speaking areas of the world.

Dr. Wang's revised set of exercises called the 18 Therapies *(Liangong shiba-fa)* is already famous, even in the West, but this is the first time his teachings of both Life-Prolonging Qigong and the 13 Grand Preservers Qigong have appeared in English.

LIFE-PROLONGING QIGONG

(Qubing-yannian ershi-shi)

The set of exercises known as Life-Prolonging Qigong, or in Chinese, *Qubing-yannian ershi-shi* (literally: "the disease-dispelling, life-prolonging 20 postures"), are made up of a simple series of movements that serve to protect the body by making it healthy and strong.

As early as several thousand years ago, China had already developed various methods of healing and treating disease, such as the use of medicinal herbs, acupuncture and moxibustion, Taoist breathing exercises, and massage. The ancient Chinese looked around themselves for hints from Nature on how to cure disease, defend themselves from attackers, and prolong their lives. They found inspiration for developing systems of preventative medicine, martial arts, and Taoist exercises in the behavior and movements of the animals around them. Sometime between the Eastern Zhou (ca. 776–256 B.C.) and the Qin (ca. 221–206 B.C.) dynasties, they developed the Two Animal Forms *(Liangqinxi),* which imitate the actions of a bear climbing a tree and hanging from its branches and a crane stretching out its wings in flight. In the Former Han dynasty (206 B.C.–A.D. 8), a third animal form—the monkey—was added. Then, over a century later, in the Later Han dynasty (A.D. 25–220) after the Three Animal Forms *(Sanqinxi)* had been strongly influenced by Taoist exercises for longevity, two more forms—based on the movements of the deer and the tiger—were added by learned doctors of medicine who developed them to help give their aristocratic patients healthier and longer lives, thus creating the Five Animal Forms *(Wuqinxi).* Since then, the Five Animal Forms have given rise to a number of forms of Qigong exercises, most notably the *Baduajin* (Eight Pieces of Silk) exercises, the *Yijinjing* (Everyday Stretching Qigong) exercises, and the internal Qi regimens of the various Shaolin and Tai-chi schools, which can all trace their ancestry back to the original Two Animal Forms and Taoist breathing exercises.

The set of Life-Prolonging Qigong given here is the version that was restored to its original form and developed by the famous proponent of Qigong Dr. Wang Ziping, who went back to the older practices such as other continuous Qigong forms for health, Tai-chi, and Taoist practices. Although it took a few decades, he was able to breathe new life into the exercises and develop the set so that it had all the effects on the body of Taoist breathing exercises and other forms of movement, including regulating and purifying the breath (and, thus, the blood), stretching and realigning the body, making possible self-massage, calming the body (nerves) and mind through meditation, unifying the inner body and the outer body, and strengthening the heart and the whole body. Dr. Wang purposely designed this new set of ancient exercises so that they could be performed by anyone—man or woman, young or old—and so that they would especially help those with the following ailments: lower-back (lumbar) problems, neck (cervical) problems, inflammation around the shoulders, inflammation of the knees, cardiovascular problems, high blood pressure, stomach and intestinal problems, chronic bronchitis, and even chronic nervous disorders.

When performing the exercises, you should start out with 3–5 repetitions, as stated in the instructions below, gradually building up to as many as 50 if you are doing this set as your main Qigong exercise.

1. Breathe Fresh Morning Air *(Shanhai zhaozhen)*

[Preparation]
Stand with the legs slightly bent and feet held about shoulders' width apart; place the right hand over the navel (or over the *dantian*, which is about 2 inches lower), and then place the left hand over the right; hold the hands there with the palms facing in (Fig. 84).

[Movement]
1. Take a deep breath, first filling the lower abdomen and then gradually filling the whole chest.

2. Then gradually exhale the breath completely. When you naturally have to take another breath, gradually take an abdominal breath, feeling the air enter the lower abdomen, This is what is called in Chinese medicine "sinking the Qi." While doing this, you should relax the whole body, stand perfectly straight (without bending the knees), close your eyes gently, touch the tip of your tongue to the ridge above the upper front teeth, and gently contract the anal sphincter. Concentrate upon the gathering of Qi, and imagine that

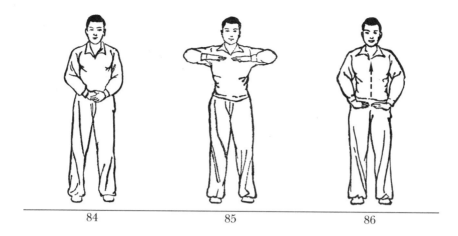

| 84 | 85 | 86 |

the Qi is purifying your body as the fresh air moves in and out. Repeat 3–5 times.

2. A Fledgling Receives Nourishment *(Youniao shoushi)*

[Preparation]
Straighten both legs, and let the arms hang naturally at your sides.

[Movement]
1. While inhaling, raise both elbows as you lift both arms such that the lower arms are almost parallel to the ground, the hands are held in front of the chest about an inch apart, and the palms are facing down (Fig. 85).

2. While exhaling, press down with the palms until the hands come to just below waist level, keeping the hands parallel to the ground and slightly bending the knees (Fig. 86).

When raising the elbows, relax the shoulders and do not let them rise up. Also, when doing this exercise, you should strive to unite your awareness, the movement, and the breath. This is a Taoist breathing technique that will help you to utilize this exercise as a method of training to promote the joining of motion and stillness.

Repeat 3–5 times.

87

3. A Giant Roc Rubs Its Craw *(Dapeng yasu)*

[Preparation]
Stand with the legs slightly bent and with the feet held about shoulders' width apart; place the right hand over the heart, and then place the left hand over the right; hold the hands there with the palms facing in (Fig. 87).

[Movement]
1. Keep the hands together, and while inhaling, gently massage the chest and upper abdomen by moving the hands in a counterclockwise circle.

2. Keep the hands together, while exhaling, gently massage the chest and upper abdomen by moving the hands in a clockwise circle.

3. Be careful not to make your circle so large that it descends to the lower abdomen. The center of the circle, where the hands are first placed in preparation for the movement, should be in the center of the body and at the base of the sternum. With each inhalation or exhalation, very gently massage the body by making one circle. Raise the head slightly, look straight ahead, and keep the upper body perfectly straight.

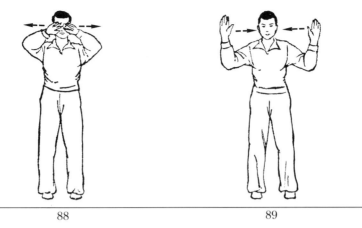

88   89

4. Making Bows to Left and Right *(Zuoyou kaigong)*

[Preparation]

Stand with the legs slightly bent and the feet held about shoulders' width apart; place both hands in front of the eyes, with the palms facing out, fingers extended, and elbows sticking out diagonally to the sides (Fig. 88).

[Movement]

1. While inhaling, move both palms (the upper arms and elbows do not move) out to the left and right, so that the palms continue to face out and the lower arms are perpendicular to the ground (Fig. 89). When they have reached that position, close the hands to form fists.

2. Then open the fists, and while exhaling, move the palms back to their position in front of the eyes.

Repeat 3–5 times.

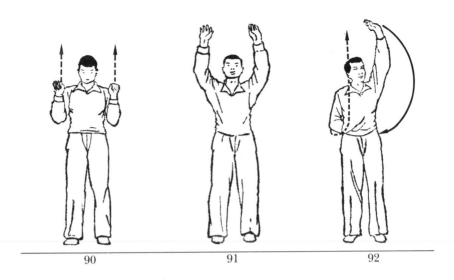

90   91   92

5. The Tyrant-King Supports the Sacrificial Vessel *(Bawang juding)*

[*Preparation*]
Stand with the legs slightly bent and with the feet held about
shoulders' width apart; bend both arms and place fists in front of
your shoulders, palms facing out (Fig. 90).

[*Movement*]
1. While inhaling, raise both arms straight up into the air; open the
hands so that the palms face up, as though supporting the weight of
a large round object (Fig. 91). Relax the shoulders and do not let
them rise; look at your hands as you raise them.
2. While exhaling, lower the arms back to their positions in front
of the shoulders, and as you do, once again form fists.
Repeat 3–5 times.

6. Pick Stars, Change Hands *(Zhaixing huandou)*

[*Preparation*]
Straighten both legs, and let the arms hang naturally at your sides.

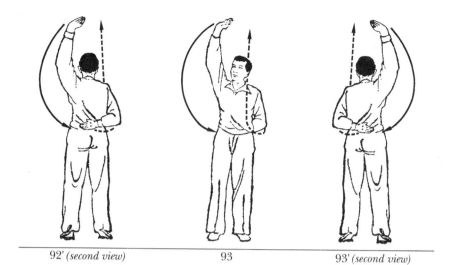

92' *(second view)* 93 93' *(second view)*

[Movement]

1. While inhaling, raise the left arm in an arc so that it comes to a stop above the head, with the palm facing up as though supporting something. Be sure to stretch the arm and shoulder completely. At the same time, swing the right arm around to the back, so that the right hand rests upon the small of the back, palm facing out. When performing this pose, look at the raised hand and allow the heels to come slightly off the ground (Figs. 92, 92'). While exhaling, bring the arms back to the preparation position.

2. While inhaling, raise the right arm in an arc so that it comes to a stop above the head, with the palm facing up as though supporting something. Be sure to stretch the arm and shoulder completely. At the same time, swing the left arm around to the back, so that the left hand rests upon the small of the back, palm facing out. When performing this pose, look at the raised hand and allow the heels to come gently back down to the ground (Figs. 93, 93'). While exhaling, bring the arms back to the preparation position.

This represents one repetition. Repeat 3–5 times.

94 95

7. A Hungry Ogre Looks in the Sea *(Nazha tanhai)*

[Preparation]
Straighten both legs, and place your hands on your waist at both sides.

[Movement]
1. While inhaling, turn the body to the right and incline downward slightly from the waist, keeping the back–neck–head straight. Look down about 2 meters (just over 2 yards) away from your feet, as though looking down into the sea from a ship or rock (Fig. 94). While exhaling, return to the preparation position.

2. While inhaling, turn the body to the left and incline downward slightly from the waist, keeping the back–neck–head all straight. Look down about 2 meters (just over 2 yards) away from your feet, as though looking down into the sea from a ship or rock (Fig. 95). While exhaling, return to the preparation position.

This represents one repetition. Repeat 3–5 times.

8. A Rhinoceros Gazes at the Moon *(Xiniu wangyue)*

[Preparation]
Straighten both legs, and place your hands on your waist at both sides.

96   97

[Movement]

1. While inhaling, turn your head to the right as far as you can. Look over your right shoulder as though trying to see the moon, which is above and behind you (Fig. 96). While exhaling, return to the preparation position.

2. While inhaling, turn your head to the left as far as you can. Look over your left shoulder as though trying to see the moon, which is above and behind you (Fig. 97). While exhaling, return to the preparation position.

This represents one repetition. Repeat 3–5 times.

> *Note:* When performing these movements, it is not necessary to turn the upper body from the waist; as much as possible, keep the upper body facing straight ahead. It will turn a little naturally; just try to hold it in position.

9. The Wind Moves the Lotus Leaf *(Fengbai heye)*

[Preparation]

Straighten both legs, and place your hands on your waist at both sides, but this time reverse the hands so that the thumbs are in front and the fingers rest on the lower back.

98   99

[*Movement*]

1. While inhaling, massage the lower back and buttock area by gently pressing with the hands and moving them up and down (Fig. 98). Then, while exhaling, swing the hips around in a clockwise circle (Fig. 99), stopping when you get back to the preparation position.

2. While inhaling, massage the lower back and buttock area by gently pressing with the hands and moving them up and down (see Fig. 98). Then, while exhaling, swing the hips around in a counterclockwise circle (*see* Fig. 99), stopping when you get back to the preparation position.

This represents one repetition. Repeat 3–5 times.

10. The Hermit Pushes Over a Stele *(Xianjen tuibei)*

[*Preparation*]

Straighten both legs, relax the shoulders, and let your arms hang naturally at your sides.

[*Movement*]

1. While inhaling, make a fist with your left hand and place it at the waist, palm up. At the same time, thrust your right arm straight out so

100   101

that it is parallel to the ground, holding the hand up as in a "Stop!" position. Simultaneously, while the body continues to face front, turn the head around to the left as far as you can, and look off straight ahead as though at distant mountains (Fig. 100). When exhaling, return the hands to your sides and face forward.

2. While inhaling, make a fist with your right hand and place it at the waist, palm up. At the same time, thrust your left arm straight out so that it is parallel to the ground, holding the hand up as in a "Stop!" position. Simultaneously, while the body continues to face front, turn the head around to the right as far as you can, and look off straight ahead as though at distant mountains (Fig. 101). When exhaling, return the hands to your sides and face forward.

This represents one repetition. Repeat 3–5 times.

11. Thrust Your Palm into the Best Haystack *(Zhangcha huashan)*

[Preparation]
Straighten both legs, relax the shoulders, and let your arms hang naturally at your sides.

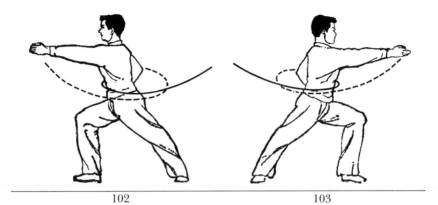

102   103

[Movement]

1. While inhaling, turn the body 90 degrees to the right; take one step forward with the right foot and fall into a Right Bow Stance. As you step into position, raise your left arm straight up in an arc and hold it at shoulder level, with the hands open and the palm facing in. At the same time, make a fist with your right hand and place it at the waist, palm up (Fig. 102). While exhaling, return to the preparation position.

2. While inhaling, turn the body 90 degrees to the left; take one step forward with the left foot and fall into a Left Bow Stance. As you step into position, raise your right arm straight up in an arc and hold it at shoulder level, with the hands open and the palm facing in. At the same time, make a fist with your left hand and place it at the waist, palm up (Fig. 103). While exhaling, return to the preparation position.

This represents one repetition. Repeat 3–5 times.

12. A White Horse Shakes Its Mane *(Baiwu fenzong)*

[Preparation]

Straighten both legs; cross the hands, and let them hang naturally in front of you.

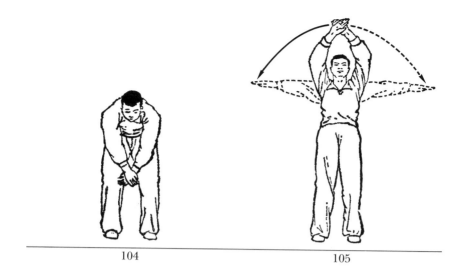

104 105

[Movement]

1. While exhaling, bend over forward so that your hands fall between your knees, which should not be allowed to bend (Fig. 104).

2. While inhaling, throw the arms up and straighten your back so that when you are standing straight your hands are directly above your head. But continue the motion—with the arms only—so that the arms fall off to each side. Hold the arms straight out at shoulder level, with the palms facing down (Fig. 105). (With the next exhalation, fall into the position shown above in Figure 104.)

This represents one repetition. Repeat 3–5 times.

13. The Wind Follows the Phoenix's Wings *(Fengfeng shunchi)*

[Preparation]

Straighten both legs, relax the shoulders, and let your arms hang naturally at your sides.

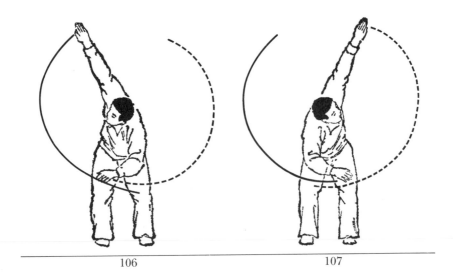

106   107

[Movement]

1. While exhaling, bend over forward, slightly bending the knees and allowing the arms to hang down loose. While inhaling, throw the right arm out and bring it up in an arc as high as it will go. At the same time, turn your head to look up at your right hand, and place your left hand on your right knee (Fig. 106).

2. While exhaling, return to the bent-over position with the knees slightly bent and the arms hanging down loose. While inhaling, throw the left arm out and bring it up in an arc as high as it will go. At the same time, turn your head to look up at your left hand, then place your right hand on your left knee (Fig. 107). (With the next exhalation, fall into the bent-over position described above for Figure 106.)

This represents one repetition. Repeat 3–5 times.

14. A Skilled Craftsman Uses a Drill *(Qiaojiang lazuan)*

[Preparation]

Straighten both legs, make fists with both hands, and place them at your sides at waist level, palms facing up.

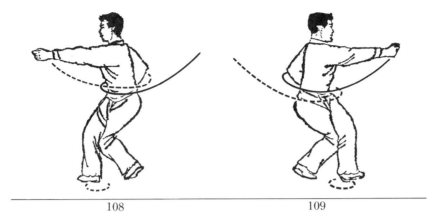

108   109

[Movement]

1. While inhaling, turn the body 90 degrees to the right; take a half-step forward with the right foot and cross it over the left foot so that the weight shifts to the right foot and your left heel comes up slightly off the ground. Your knees should be locked together. As you step into position, push out with the left fist so that the arm rises to shoulder level; while "punching," turn the fist so that it rests with the palm facing in (Fig. 108). During this movement, keep your right fist at the waist, palm up. While exhaling, return to the preparation position.

2. While inhaling, turn the body 90 degrees to the left; take a half-step forward with the left foot, and cross it over the right foot so that the weight shifts to the left foot and your right heel comes up slightly off the ground. Your knees should be locked together. As you step into position, push out with the right fist so that the arm rises to shoulder level; while "punching," turn the fist so that it rests with the palm facing in (Fig. 109). During this movement, keep your left fist at the waist, palm up. While exhaling, return to the preparation position.

This represents one repetition. Repeat 3–5 times.

15. A Green Dragon Leaps and Turns *(Qinglong tengquan)*

[Preparation]

Straighten both legs, relax the shoulders, and let your arms hang naturally at your sides.

[Movement]

1. While inhaling, do the following: make a fist with your left hand and place it by your side at waist level with the palm facing up; take a step 90 degrees to the left with your left foot, fall into a Left Half-bow Stance (notice that the right foot continues to point in the original direction and does not shift), and turn the upper body to the left; raise the right arm to shoulder level and hold it straight out, the hand standing so that the palm faces out (Fig. 110). After falling into the pose, slowly exhale.

2. Then, while inhaling, open up the left hand and extend the arm; start to raise both arms up in arcs (Fig. 111). When both arms are pointing straight up, you should have twisted your body so that it faces forward again (Fig. 112). While exhaling, bend forward, trying not to bend the knees, and let the arms hang loose (Fig. 113).

Then, as you inhale, do the following simultaneously: make a fist with your right hand and place it by your side at waist level, with the palm facing up; take a step 90 degrees to the right with your right foot, fall into a Right Half-bow Stance and turn the upper body to the right; raise the left arm to shoulder level and hold it straight out, the hand standing so that the palm faces out (Fig. 114). After falling into the pose, slowly exhale.

3. Then, while inhaling, open up the right hand and extend the arm; start to raise both arms up in arcs (Fig. 115). When both arms are pointing straight up, you should have twisted your body so that it faces forward again (Fig. 116). While exhaling, bend forward, trying not to bend the knees, and let the arms hang loose (Fig. 117).

This represents one repetition. Repeat 3–5 times.

Note: Throughout these movements, the eyes should follow the movement of the hands.

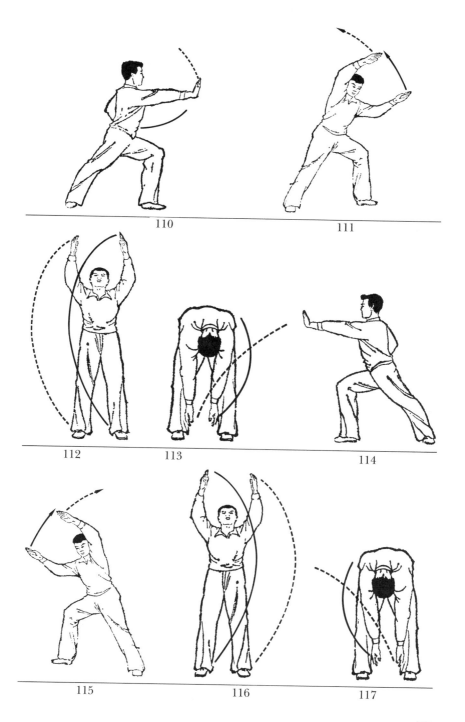

110

111

112 113

114

115 116 117

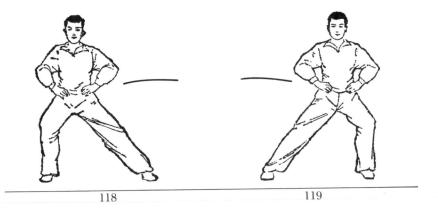

118   119

16. A Talkative Man, a Sleeping Dog *(Luohan fuquan)*

[Preparation]
Straighten both legs, face forward, and place your hands on your waist at both sides. This time, stand with the feet about 2 shoulders' widths apart.

[Movement]
   1. While inhaling, bend the right knee and keep the left leg straight, shifting your weight to the right (Fig. 118). While exhaling, return to the preparation position.
   2. While inhaling, bend the left knee and keep the right leg straight, shifting your weight to the left (Fig. 119). While exhaling, return to the preparation position.
   This represents one repetition. Repeat 3–5 times.

17. A White Crane Swirls Its Knees *(Baihe quanxi)*

[Preparation]
From the preparation position, gently bend both knees; bend over forward and place both hands on your knees (Fig. 120). You should continue to look straight ahead, with fingers pointing straight down the front of your legs.

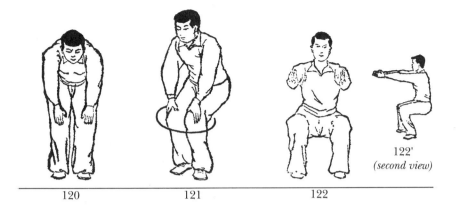

122'
(second view)

120   121   122

[Movement]

1. While inhaling, straighten the back as much as possible, turn the hands so that the fingers move to the outside of your legs, and swirl your knees around first in a clockwise circle (Fig. 121) and then in a counterclockwise circle. When you finish these circles, relax your back while exhaling and return to the position shown in Figure 120.

This represents one repetition. Repeat 3–5 times.

18. The Taoist Ascetic Sits Down *(Xingzhe xiazuo)*

[Preparation]

Straighten both legs, hold the feet about shoulders' width apart, relax the shoulders, and let your arms hang naturally at your sides.

[Movement]

1. While inhaling, slowly sink into a deep squat; at the same time, raise both arms straight up and out so that they are at shoulder level and the fingers of the hands point out, with the palms facing in (Figs. 122, 122'). Be sure to keep the back straight, and try to position the thighs so they are parallel to the floor. If that position is too deep for you, do what is comfortable, gradually working your way to the deeper pose.

2. While exhaling, slowly rise up into the preparation position, dropping your arms back to your sides.

This represents one repetition. Repeat 3–5 times.

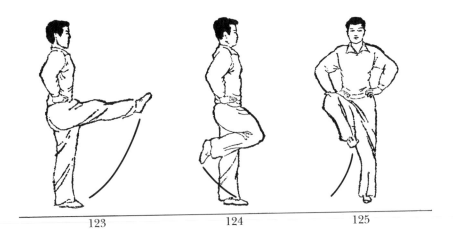

123   124   125

19. The White Lotus Sways in Four Directions *(Simian bailian)*

[Preparation]

Straighten both legs, hold the feet about shoulders' width apart, relax the shoulders, and place your hands on your hips.

[Movement]

1. While inhaling, swing the right leg up so that it is parallel to the ground and at a 90-degree angle to the body; while swinging the leg, point the toes (Fig. 123); while exhaling, drop the leg back to the ground. Then, while inhaling, raise the left leg in the same way, dropping it while exhaling.

2. While inhaling, pick up the right leg slightly and kick back with the heel (Fig. 124); while exhaling, drop the leg. Then, while inhaling, raise the left leg in the same way, dropping it while exhaling.

3. While inhaling, raise the right knee as far as you can, straight up and pointing a little to the outside, and keep the sole of the right foot almost on the left leg (Fig. 125); while exhaling, drop the leg. Then, while inhaling, raise the left knee in the same way, dropping it while exhaling.

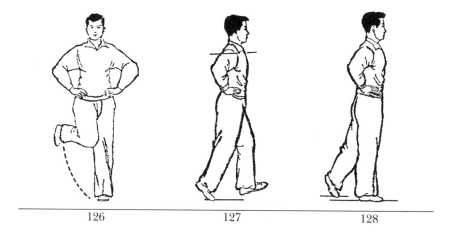

| 126 | 127 | 128 |

4. While inhaling, bend the right leg backward at the knee, raising the foot back and to the side (Fig. 126); while exhaling, drop the leg. Then, while inhaling, bend the left leg backward and raise the left foot in the same way, dropping it while exhaling.

This represents one repetition. Repeat 3–5 times.

20. A Hermit Paces Back and Forth *(Xianzong paihui)*

[Preparation]
Straighten both legs, hold the feet about shoulders' width apart, relax the shoulders, and place your hands on your hips.

[Movement]
1. While inhaling, step forward with the left foot, placing the left heel only on the ground; stand up straight and do not bend the knees, letting the heel of the right foot come up off the ground (Fig. 127).

2. While exhaling, place the left foot firmly on the ground and step forward with the right foot, placing all your weight upon the right leg and standing straight (Fig. 128).

3. While inhaling, step forward with the left foot; as you place the left heel on the ground, slightly bend the right knee (Fig. 129).

4. With the weight still on the bent right leg, and while exhaling, turn the left ankle down so that only the toes of the left foot touch the ground and you are supporting all of your weight on the right foot (Fig. 130).

5. While inhaling, place the left foot firmly on the ground and step forward with the right foot, placing the right heel on the ground and bending the left knee slightly (Fig. 131). While exhaling, return to the preparation position.

6. While inhaling, step forward with the right foot, placing the right heel only on the ground; stand up straight and do not bend the knees, letting the heel of the left foot come up off the ground (Fig. 132).

7. While exhaling, place the right foot firmly on the ground (Fig. 133) and step forward with the left foot, placing all your weight upon the left leg and standing straight .

8. While inhaling, step forward with the right foot; as you place the right heel on the ground (as in Fig. 132), slightly bend the left knee (Fig. 134).

9. With the weight still on the bent left leg, and while exhaling, turn the right ankle down so that only the toes of the right foot touch the ground and you are supporting all of your weight on the left foot (Fig. 135).

10. While inhaling, place the right foot firmly on the ground and step forward with the left foot, placing the left heel on the ground and bending the right knee slightly (Fig. 136). While exhaling, return to the preparation position.

This represents one repetition. Repeat 3–5 times.

You have now completed the Life-Prolonging Qigong set.

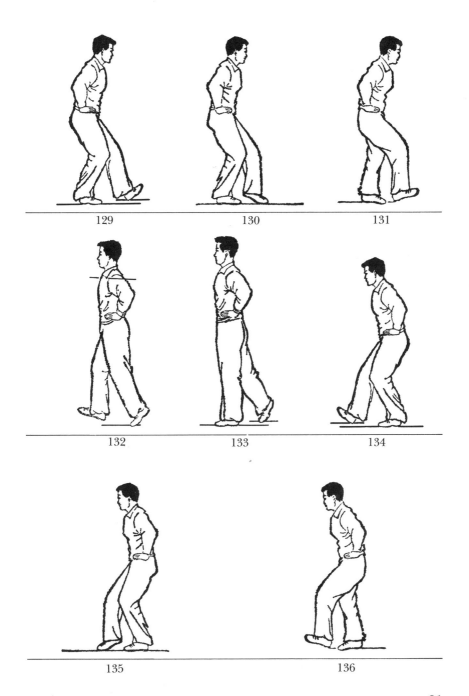

129   130   131

132   133   134

135   136

THE THIRTEEN GRAND PRESERVERS

(Shisan taibao-gong)

The Qigong set given here, the 13 Grand Preservers (*Shisan taibao-gong*), appears to be founded upon an ancient system of Taoist breathing exercises to which have been added the benefits of Qigong practices developed from the various internal martial arts.

Once, the teaching of this form of Qigong was a secret, man-to-man transmission of the art. Thus, for many centuries, even the existence of the 13 Grand Preservers set was not known. But one teacher in the direct transmission lineage, Dr. Wang Ziping, passed the secret teachings of the form to a few people, starting in about 1965. Since that time, it not only survived the Cultural Revolution but even went on to gain great popularity in the Chinese-speaking areas of the world.

The fundamental characteristics of this secret teaching for health and longevity are as follows:

1. It helps in achieving and maintaining a straight and flexible spinal column, which is essential for a long and healthy life.
2. It uses a method of holding certain poses, which stretches and rejuvenates all of the body's muscles and tendons.
3. It also uses a walking method, which serves to increase the efficiency of the circulation and also to keep the lower back and legs supple and limber.

Therefore, in order for you to obtain the greatest benefit from these poses, you should be careful to:

1. Always stand perfectly straight, with the backbone straight from the tip of the head to the tailbone (coccyx), the pelvic girdle slightly tipped backward (like a dog with its tail between its legs), the anal sphincter slightly contracted, and the tip of the tongue lightly placed on the ridge above the upper teeth.
2. Feel that your feet are rooted to the ground, whence you can draw energy, and also that your head is being pulled up into the clouds; in other words, your body should feel both heavy and light at the same time.

137 PREPARATION POSITION

3. Breathe according to the instructions given, matching your inhalations and exhalations to the movements in as natural a manner as possible.
4. Calm the mind and relax the body before starting.
5. Try to achieve a union of the outer Qi and your inner Qi.

Note: These exercises are intended for the use of anyone who is already in fairly good health, and who wants to become even healthier and live longer. Middle-aged and elderly persons should only perform these exercises if they are able to do them without any strain. If there is any pain, they should discontinue practicing them immediately. If there is any doubt about whether or not you are healthy enough to undertake these exercises, please consult your doctor before attempting to practice them.

1. A Tiger Sleeps in the Nanshan Peaks *(Nanshan fuhu)*

[Preparation]

Stand up straight, heels together, each foot pointing out 45 degrees. Make fists with both hands and hold them at your sides at waist level, palms facing up (Fig. 137).

138   139

[Movement]

1. While inhaling, take a large step with the right foot directly to the side; the left foot, which stays in place, should shift slightly so that the toes point straight ahead, while the right foot should point directly to the right. (The right leg is bent so that the thigh is almost parallel to the ground, and the left leg is held very straight.) At the same time, raise the right hand straight up so that the right arm is held in an arc and the fist is held vertically, with the thumb on the top and knuckles facing front. Simultaneously lower the left fist so that the left arm also forms a gentle arc, with the left fist held before the *dantian,* palm facing in (Fig. 138).

2. While exhaling, return to the preparation position.

3. While inhaling, take a large step with the left foot directly to the side; the right foot, which stays in place, should shift slightly so that the toes point straight ahead, while the left foot should point directly to the left. (The left leg is bent so that the thigh is almost parallel to the ground, and the right leg is held very straight.) At the same time, raise the left hand straight up so that the left arm is held in an arc and the fist is held vertically, with the thumb on the top and knuckles facing front. Simultaneously lower the right fist so that the right arm also forms a gentle arc, with the right fist held before the *dantian,* palm facing in (Fig. 139).

This represents one repetition. Repeat 3–5 times.

84 • CHAPTER 2

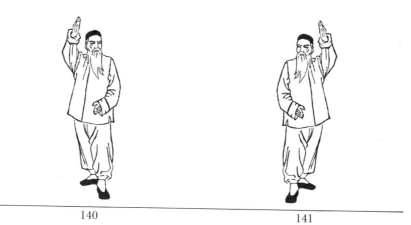

140   141

2. A Dragon Dives into the Arctic Sea *(Beihai jianglong)*

[Preparation]

Stand up straight, heels together, each foot pointing out 45 degrees.
Make fists with both hands and hold them at your sides at waist level,
palms facing up.

[Movement]

1. While inhaling, take a half-step forward with the left foot so that
only the toes of the left foot touch the ground. The right foot does
not change its position or orientation, and the left toes are aligned
with the right heel. At the same time, raise the right hand straight up
so that the right arm points straight up and the right hand opens into
a palm facing back. Simultaneously lower the left hand, also opened
into a palm, so that the left arm also forms a gentle arc, with the left
palm held before the *dantian,* facing in (Fig. 140).

2. While exhaling, return to the preparation position.

3. While inhaling, take a half-step forward with the right foot so
that only the toes of the right foot touch the ground. The left foot
does not change its position or orientation, and the right toes are
aligned with the left heel. At the same time, raise the left hand
straight up so that the left arm points straight up and the left hand
opens into a palm facing back. Simultaneously lower the right hand,
also opened into a palm, so that the right arm also forms a gentle arc,
with the right palm held before the *dantian,* facing in (Fig. 141).

142   143   144

4. While exhaling, return to the preparation position.
This represents one repetition. Repeat 3–5 times.

3. A Golden Dragon Shuts Its Mouth *(Jinlong hekou)*

[Preparation]
Stand up straight, heels together, each foot pointing out 45 degrees. Make fists with both hands and hold them at your sides at waist level, palms facing up.

[Movement]
1. While inhaling, take a small step to the right with the right foot (the toes still pointing out 45 degrees). At the same time, place the hands in front of the chest and join the tips of all five fingers, raising the elbows so that the arms are almost parallel to the ground (Fig. 142). Do this during the first half of your breath, and in the second half, as you move your hands directly to the left as far as you can, turn your head as far as possible to the right (Fig. 143).
2. While exhaling, return to the preparation position.
3. While inhaling, take a small step to the left with the left foot (the

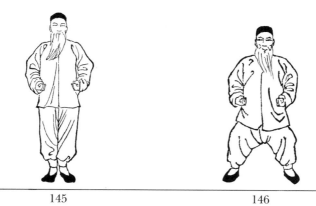

145   146

toes still pointing out 45 degrees). At the same time, place the hands in front of the chest and join the tips of all 5 fingers, raising the elbows so that the arms are almost parallel to the ground (*see* Fig. 142). Do this during the first half of your breath, and in the second half, as you move your hands directly to the right as far as you can, simultaneously turn your head as far as possible to the left (Fig. 144).

4. While exhaling, return to the preparation position.

This represents one repetition. Repeat 3–5 times.

4. A Sparrow Hawk Seizes Its Prey *(Yaoying zhushi)*

[Preparation]

Stand up straight, heels together, each foot pointing out 45 degrees. Make fists with both hands and hold them at your sides at waist level, palms facing up (Fig. 145).

2. While exhaling, take a step to the right with the right foot, falling into a Horse-riding Stance (the feet should be about two shoulders' widths apart), keeping the upper body straight but dropping your center of gravity (Fig. 146).

147   148

[Movement]

1. While inhaling, turn the body to face 45 degrees to the left and thrust out the right hand (which is now opened into a palm) so that the arm, which is held at shoulder level, points diagonally to the left and the palm faces down (Fig. 147). Do this during the first half of your breath. During the second half, turn the body 90 degrees to the right (from that position); at the same time, swing the arm around (at shoulder level) so that it points diagonally to the right; but this time turn the palm so that it faces up (Fig. 148).

2. While exhaling, turn the body back to face front and draw the right hand back in toward the waist, "closing your talons" (Fig. 149) and changing it into a fist along the way. You should finish in the position shown in Figure 146.

3. While inhaling, turn the body to face 45 degrees to the right and thrust out the left hand (which is now opened into a palm) so that the arm, which is held at shoulder level, points diagonally to the right and the palm faces down (Fig. 150). Do this during the first half of your breath. During the second half, turn the body 90 degrees to the left (from that position); at the same time, swing the arm around (at shoulder level) so that it points diagonally to the left; but this time turn the palm so that it faces up (Fig. 151).

4. While exhaling, turn the body back to face front and withdraw

149   150

151   152

the left hand back to the waist, "closing your talons" (Fig. 152) and changing it into a fist along the way. You should finish in the position shown in Figure 146.

This represents one repetition. Repeat 3–5 times.

5. Diamond-Bright Arms *(Jingang-liang bi)*

[Preparation]

Continue from the Horse-riding Stance you returned to at the end of Posture 4.

[Movement]

1. While inhaling, punch straight out and up with the right fist so that the arm points directly away from and is aligned in front of the right shoulder (Fig 153). Be certain to rotate the fist while punching, so that at the end the thumb is on the bottom, and be careful not to punch too high or too low (Fig. 154).

2. Return to the Horse-riding Stance

3. While inhaling, punch straight out and up with the left fist so that the arm points directly away from and is aligned in front of the left shoulder (Fig 155). Be certain to rotate the fist while punching, so that at the end the thumb is on the bottom, and be careful not to punch too high or too low (Fig. 156).

4. Return to the Horse-riding Stance.

This represents one repetition. Repeat 3–5 times.

6. Finally Thrusting the Golden Spears *(Jiuzha jinqiang)*

[Preparation]

Stand up straight, heels together, each foot pointing out 45 degrees. Make fists with both hands and hold them at your sides at waist level, palms facing up (Fig. 157).

[Movement]

1. While inhaling, turn the body 90 degrees to the right and step forward with the right foot, falling into a Right Bow Stance (Fig. 158). At the same time, punch straight out and up with both fists so that they end up at shoulder height, palms facing in (Fig. 159).

2. While exhaling, return to the preparation position.

3. While inhaling, turn the body 90 degrees to the left and step forward with the left foot, falling into a Left Bow Stance (Fig. 160). At the same time, punch straight out and up with both fists so that they end up at shoulder height, palms facing in (Fig. 161).

4. While exhaling, return to the preparation position.

This represents one repetition. Repeat 3–5 times.

153

154

155

156

157

158

159

160

161

162

7. Draw Your Bow, Shoot the Vulture *(Kaigong shediao)*

[Preparation]

Stand up straight, heels together, each foot pointing out 45 degrees. Make fists with both hands and hold them at your sides at waist level, palms facing up (Fig. 162).

[Movement]

1. While inhaling, and without moving the lower body, twist the upper torso to face left, raising the arms so that the left arm is straight and points to the left at shoulder level (the left fist is held as though holding a bow) and the right arm is held so that the fist is held (as if drawing the bowstring) near the left armpit (Fig. 163). At the same time, step to the right with the right foot, falling into a Rear Right Bow Stance, in which the right leg is rather bent and the left leg is almost straight (Fig 164).

2. While exhaling, return to the preparation position.

3. While inhaling, and without moving the lower body, twist the upper torso to face to the right, raising the arms so that the right arm is straight and points to the right at shoulder level (the right fist held as though holding a bow) and the left arm is held so that the fist is held (as if drawing the bowstring) near the right armpit (Fig. 165). At

163   164

165   166

the same time, step to the left with the left foot, falling into a Rear Left Bow Stance, in which the left leg is rather bent and the right leg is almost straight (Fig. 166).

4. While exhaling, return to the preparation position.

This represents one repetition. Repeat 3–5 times.

8. A Palm Divides the Flowery Mound *(Zhangpi huashan)*

[Preparation]

Stand up straight, heels together, each foot pointing out 45 degrees. Make fists with both hands and hold them at your sides at waist level, palms facing up (*see* Fig. 162).

167	168	169

[*Movement*]

1. While inhaling, open the left hand into a palm and place it in front of the right-hand edge of the chest; open the right hand into a palm and swing it in a large arc to the back, palm facing in; when the arm points straight up, start exhaling, turn the palm to face out and bring the arm all the way around so that the hand comes to rest beside the bent knee of the right leg, with which you have taken a half-step forward, placing it so that only the toes touch the ground (Fig. 167). You should be looking at your right hand.

2. While inhaling, step forward with the right foot and fall into a Right Bow Stance. At the same time, turn the right palm over to face in and raise the right arm so that it points off to the right and up; drop the left arm so the left palm rests just above the left thigh, palm down. As you are moving into this pose, turn the head to the left as far as you can, as though trying to look behind you (Fig. 168).

3. While exhaling, return to the preparation position.

4. While inhaling, open the right hand into a palm and place it in front of the left-hand edge of the chest; open the left hand into a palm and swing it in a large arc to the back, palm facing in; when the arm points straight up, start exhaling, turn the palm to face out and bring the arm all the way around so that the hand comes to rest

170   171

beside the bent knee of the left leg, with which you have taken a half-step forward, placing it so that only the toes touch the ground (Fig. 169). You should be looking at your left hand.

4. While inhaling, step forward with the left foot and fall into a Left Bow Stance. At the same time, turn the left palm over to face in and raise the left arm so that it points off to the left and up; and drop the right arm so that the right palm rests just above the right thigh, palm down. As you are moving into this pose, turn the head to the right as far as you can, as though trying to look behind you (Fig. 170).

5. While exhaling, return to the preparation position.

This represents one repetition. Repeat 3–5 times.

9. The Night Flight of a Spear *(Ye xingfei piao)*

[Preparation]
Stand up straight, heels together, each foot pointing out 45 degrees. Make fists with both hands and hold them at your sides at waist level, palms facing up (Fig. 171).

[Movement]

1. While inhaling, take a large step to the side with the right foot, bending the right knee and keeping the left leg straight; at the same time, drop the left fist so that it stops about 15 cm above the left thigh, open the right hand and move it in front of the navel area, palm down, and turn the head to look off to the far left (Fig. 172). Note that both feet are still pointing out 45 degrees.

2. While exhaling, turn the right foot so that the toes point directly to the right; while doing so, bend the right knee even more and let the left foot turn so that the toes point straight ahead. At the same time, raise the right hand so that it points to the right and up, but this time turn the wrist so that the fingers point up (Fig. 173).

3. While inhaling, turn the right hand over so that the palm points up and out. At the same time, fall even deeper into the stance, allowing the left knee to bend a little if necessary, and bend the left arm, turning the left fist so that the wrist is bent, the fist is pulled in, and the palm faces down (Fig. 174).

4. While exhaling, return to the preparation position (Fig. 175).

5. While inhaling, take a large step to the side with the left foot, bending the left knee and keeping the right leg straight; at the same time, drop the right fist so that it stops about 15 cm above the right thigh, open the left hand and move it in front of the navel area, palm down, and turn the head to look far off to the right (Fig. 176). Note that both feet are still pointing out 45 degrees.

6. While exhaling, turn the left foot so that the toes point directly to the left; while doing so, bend the left knee even more and let the right foot turn so that the toes point straight ahead. At the same time, raise the left hand so that it points to the left and up, but this time turn the wrist so that the fingers point up (Fig. 177).

7. While inhaling, turn the left hand over so that the palm points up and out. At the same time, fall even deeper into the stance, allowing the right knee to bend a little if necessary, and bend the right arm, turning the right fist so that the wrist is bent, the fist is pulled in, and the palm faces down (Fig. 178).

8. While exhaling, return to the preparation position.

This represents one repetition. Repeat 3–5 times.

| 172 | 173 | 174 |

| 175 | 176 |

| 177 | 178 |

10. The Boatman Shoulders a Towline *(Zhoufu beiqian)*

[Preparation]

Stand up straight, heels together, each foot pointing out 45 degrees. Make fists with both hands and hold them at your sides at waist level, palms facing up (Fig. 179).

[Movement]

1. While inhaling, take a small step to the right with the right foot and extend both arms out to the sides, holding them at shoulder level, thumbs facing down (Fig. 180). Do this during the first half of your breath. During the second half, twist the whole body to the left as far as you can; at the same time, place the right fist beside the right ear, thumb facing out, and return the left fist to the waist (thumb up). Slightly incline the body forward so that the line from your head to your right foot is straight, and look as far to the left as possible (Fig. 181).

2. While exhaling, return to the pose shown in Figure 180.

3. While inhaling, twist the whole body to the right as far as you can; at the same time, place the left fist beside the left ear, thumb facing out, and return the right fist to the waist (thumb up). Slightly incline the body forward so that the line from your head to your left foot is straight, and look as far to the right as possible (Fig. 182).

4. While exhaling, return to the preparation position.

This represents one repetition. Repeat 3–5 times.

11. Lift Up Half a Ton *(Lituo qianjin)*

Note that although based on an ancient Chinese form, this movement greatly resembles the squat-and-jerk style of weight lifting.

[Preparation]

1. Stand up straight, heels together, each foot pointing out 45 degrees. Make fists with both hands and hold them at your sides at waist level, palms facing up (Fig. 183).

2. Take a step to the right with the right foot (Fig. 184).

179 180

181 182

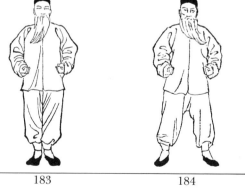

183 184

185   186

187   187' *(second view)*

[*Movement*]

1. While inhaling, raise both fists to shoulder level, thumbs facing out (Fig. 185).

2. While exhaling, sink down into a deep knee bend; at the same time, extend both arms straight up into the air (Fig. 186).

3. While inhaling, stand back up as though returning to the preparation position, dropping your fists back to shoulder level; but take a step forward with your right foot and fall into a Right Bow Stance (Figs. 187, 187').

4. While exhaling, sink deeper into the Right Bow Stance by bending the right knee even more; at the same time extend both arms as though punching diagonally up, so that the line from the fists to the left heel is straight (Figs. 188, 188').

188   188' *(second view)*   189   189' *(second view)*

190   190' *(second view)*

5. While inhaling, return to the pose shown in Figure 185.

6. While exhaling, sink down into a deep knee bend; at the same time, extend both arms straight up into the air.

7. While inhaling, stand back up as though returning to the pose shown in Figure 185, dropping your fists back to shoulder level; but instead take a step forward with your left foot and fall into a Left Bow Stance (Figs. 189, 189').

8. While exhaling, sink deeper into the Left Bow Stance by bending the left knee even more; at the same time extend both arms as though punching diagonally up, so that the line from the fists to the right heel is straight (Figs. 190, 190').

9. Return to the preparation position.

This represents one repetition. Repeat 3–5 times.

12. The Monkey's Hand Pokes Its Arm *(Yuanshou tongbi)*

[Preparation]

1. Stand up straight, heels together, each foot pointing out 45 degrees. Make fists with both hands and hold them at your sides at waist level, palms facing up (Fig. 191).

2. Take a large step to the right with the right foot.

[Movement]

1. While inhaling, open the right hand into a palm, and turning your body first to the right, draw an arc with the right arm that goes first behind you. As it comes to its zenith, turn the body to face diagonally to the left as far as you can, and let the arm continue in its arc until it comes to rest just above shoulder level, pointing off diagonally to the left (Fig. 192). During all of this, the left fist stays at the waist.

2. While exhaling, shift the weight back to the right leg (Fig. 193), and keep moving, twisting the body back to the right and dropping the arm so that the right palm rests upon the right thigh; but before the palm reaches the thigh, shift the weight again so that the left leg supports the body (Fig. 194). The eyes should look off to the right side.

3. Return to part 2 of the preparation position

4. While inhaling, raise both arms high above the head, crossing them, with the right hand in front (both palms facing out) and the eyes looking up at the hands (Fig. 195).

5. While exhaling, bend the knees, falling into a shallow Horse-riding Stance, and drop the arms in arcs, always looking at the right hand (Fig. 196). Continue to arc the arms until the hands come beneath the thighs. Your eyes should be looking down at the right knee (Fig. 197).

6. Return to part 2 of the preparation position

7. While inhaling, open the left hand into a palm, and turning your body first to the left, draw an arc with the left arm that goes first behind you; as it comes to its zenith, turn the body to face diagonally to the right as far as you can, and let the arm continue in its arc until it comes to rest just above shoulder level, pointing off diagonally to the right (Fig. 198). During all of this, the right fist stays at the waist.

191

192

193

194

195

196

197

198

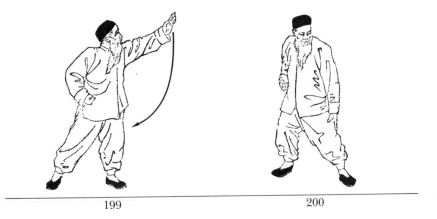

199   200

8. While exhaling, shift the weight back to the left leg (Fig. 199), and keep moving, twisting the body back to the left and dropping the arm so that the left palm rests upon the left thigh; but before the palm reaches the thigh, shift the weight again so that the right leg supports the body (Fig. 200). The eyes should look off to the left side.

9. Return to part 2 of the preparation position.

10. While inhaling, raise both arms high above the head, crossing them, with the left hand in front (both palms facing out) and the eyes looking up at the hands (Fig. 201).

11. While exhaling, bend the knees, falling into a shallow Horse-riding Stance, and drop the arms in arcs, always looking at the left hand (Fig. 202). Continue to arc the arms until the hands come beneath the thighs. Your eyes should be looking down at the left knee (Fig. 203).

12. Return to the preparation position.

This represents one repetition. Repeat 3–5 times.

13. Brandish a Weapon and Split a Stone *(Lunwu shijue)*

Note that in order to make these directions easier to follow, for this series of movements we shall designate the direction in which you are facing when beginning as north; thus, east is to the right; south, to the rear; and west, to the left when you start. We shall give compass directions to avoid confusion.

201   202   203

204   205

[Preparation]

1. Stand up straight, facing north, heels together, each foot pointing out 45 degrees. Make fists with both hands and hold them at your sides at waist level, palms facing up (Fig. 204).

2. Keeping the feet together, raise the right arm straight out to the side (east), with the back of the fist to the back, and raise the left arm so that the fist is in front of the left edge of the chest, the thumb facing in. At the same time, turn the head to face directly right (Fig. 205).

| 206 | 207 |

[Movement]

1. While inhaling, step to the northwest with the left foot (toes still pointing out 45 degrees), and bend the left knee, letting the right foot shift to point north (Fig. 206). Do this during the first half of your breath. During the second half, turn the body to face northwest. At the same time, swing the left fist over in an arc so that you look like you have executed a left punch at shoulder level (Fig. 207). Your eyes should follow the left fist, which should be vertical at the end.

2. While exhaling, step forward (northwest) with the right foot and turn the body around 180 degrees (to face southeast), pivoting on the ball of the right foot and the heel of the left foot. As you do, drop your fists and cross your wrists before your navel, the right wrist on the outside (thumbs facing in), and turn the head to look off to your left, making sure the knees are bent and the weight is on the left leg (Figs. 208, 208').

3. While inhaling, raise the right foot so that only the toes touch the ground; at the same time, pivot to face northwest, thrust both arms out, and form a cross with your body, keeping both fists vertical (Fig. 209).

4. While exhaling, place the right foot down and swing the arms so that as the right arm comes into the chest the left arm swings up and around 360 degrees. Turn your head to face left at the same time,

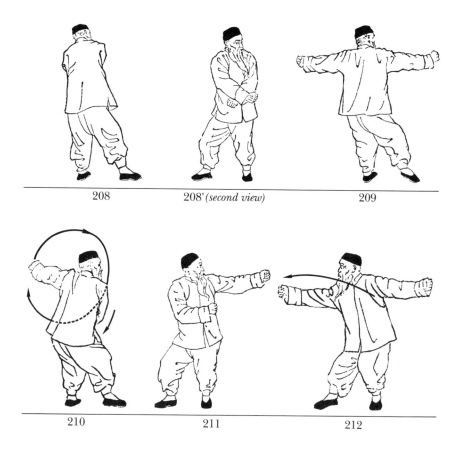

208   208' *(second view)*   209

210   211   212

and make a left-sided version of the pose in Figure 206, making sure your front (right) knee is bent (Figs. 210, 211).

5. While inhaling, turn the body to face northwest; at the same time, swing the right fist over in an arc so that you look like you have executed a right punch at shoulder level (Fig. 212). Your eyes should follow the right fist, which should be vertical at the end.

213   214

6. While exhaling, step forward (northwest) with the left foot and turn the body around 180 degrees (to face southeast), pivoting on the ball of the left foot and the heel of the right foot. As you do, drop your fists and cross your wrists before your navel, the left wrist on the outside (thumbs facing in), and turn the head to look off to your right, making sure the knees are bent and the weight is on the right leg (Figs. 213, 214).

7. While inhaling, raise the left foot so that only the toes touch the ground; at the same time, pivot to face northwest, thrust both arms out, and form a cross with your body, keeping both fists vertical (Fig. 215).

8. While exhaling, place the left foot down and swing the arms so that as the left arm comes into the chest the right arm swings up and around 360 degrees. Turn your head to face right at the same time, and make the pose shown in Figure 209, making sure your front (left) knee is bent (Figs. 216, 217).

9. Return to the preparation position (Fig. 218).

This represents one repetition. Repeat 3–5 times.

You have now completed the 13 Grand Preservers set.

215

216

217

218 PREPARATION POSITION

3

Preventative Forms (Baozhi-gong)

PRINCIPLES

The original meaning of the word Qigong is "breathing exercises," which we will introduce in this chapter. Through Qigong training, you can gain physical and mental benefits by regulating the breath. To do this, you must imagine that when you inhale air, you are actually inhaling essential Qi from Nature. To take deep breaths is to take in and give off large amounts of oxygen and carbon dioxide, respectively. Just in terms of the actual physical processes that go on when we breathe, respiration involves an exchange of gases in the blood stream. Air is taken into the lungs, where it interacts with capillaries connected to the pulmonary circulatory system. There the hemoglobin in the blood gives off carbon dioxide, a product of the body's various chemical reactions, and collects fresh oxygen, which then passes throughout the body where it is exchanged for carbon dioxide. Thus we can see that there is a close connection between the respiratory and the circulatory systems. The circulation is, of course, controlled by the heart.

But Chinese medicine teaches that a body cannot be completely well unless the lung-Qi flows without obstruction. According to Chinese traditional teachings, the lungs function as follows: water in the stomach travels through the spleen to the lungs; together with descending lung-Qi, the water descends to the kidneys; the impurities in the water are expelled from the body through the bladder, and the pure essence is distilled into vital Qi by the Triple Heater and sent up to the lungs, where it is circulated and transformed into water which is sent to the kidneys. Thus, in this circulation system—which maintains the body's fluid balance—the kidneys store the vital Qi. This vital Qi can be supplemented through the diligent practice of Qigong.

There are six basic methods of regulating the breath in Qigong: exhalation, inhalation, deep exhalation, breath-retention, blowing, and aspirating. *Inhalation* and *exhalation* refer to "normal breathing," which, for any student of Qigong, means abdominal breathing. This type of breathing is conducive to having a relaxed body and a tranquil mind. *Deep exhalation* is a method whereby one expels air deeply through the mouth, and takes in air less deeply. Deep exhaling can activate the parasympathetic nervous system and thereby help to dilate the blood vessels, lower the blood pressure, and even lower cholesterol levels. *Breath-retention* is a method of holding the breath; it is practiced in order to cleanse the body more thoroughly and is thought to be very good for nervous disorders. *Blowing* is a type of shallow breathing in and out through the nose. Being nasal breathing, the inhaled air is purified and warmed by the nasal tract, which is beneficial to the lungs. As it also stimulates the pineal and the pituitary glands, the "third eye" and the endocrine system are in turn stimulated. *Aspirating* is a type of breathing in which the practitioner pronounces certain Chinese sounds thought to stimulate certain organs as described in the millenniums-old *Huang-di neijing* (The Yellow Emperor's Classic of Internal Medicine).

Another type of practice, and the one we would like to end with, is a method of maintaining health by performing self-massage to stimulate the 5 organs. Since prehistoric times, people have probably rubbed and massaged sore muscles and painful areas of the body. The different people of the globe have all developed their own forms of massage, but the Chinese system was devised according to the theory of Qi circulation throughout the body. There are 3 types of Chinese massage: massaging the muscle; massaging the related acupuncture points; and rubbing or pressing down (shiatsu) upon the endings of nerves and Qi meridians. The exercises given here can be used daily to help invigorate the internal organs and thus lead to better health and a longer life.

BREATHING EXERCISES

(Qi-gong)

The exercises that follow can be done in any comfortable position—sitting, standing, or even lying down; the only thing you have to do is relax and close the eyes. Here we present seven exercises that we feel are of the greatest benefit in helping modern-day working people to relax both mentally and physically.

Preparation

Before beginning to do any of these exercises, make sure that you have not eaten for about an hour, for they could upset digestion. Do not do them when sleepy, as you will probably fall asleep.

At first, make yourself comfortable, and make sure that your clothing is not too tight around the waist. Take 3–5 deep breaths to relax, and then begin. You may do any one of the exercises given, jump around and combine a few, or do them all in sequence, as you like. At first, you will probably want to do these exercises for no more than a few minutes each, as instructed below. As you become more proficient, you may want to experiment with lengthening the time until you find an exercise or a time that feels good.

1. Normal Breathing

This is the first stage of qi-gong breathing exercises. After you have relaxed, if you are a chest breather, gradually change to abdominal breathing. Try to make the change in the mind first, and then the breath will follow. The breaths should be slow, long, and even.

When doing these breathing exercises, unless instructed otherwise, imagine your Qi to be centered around the *Mingmen* point (on the middle of the back, at the waist; check the positions of the points named in these exercises in Figs. 1–12, pp. 10–13).

Now, inhale through the nose deeply and slowly, and while you do, allow the air to first inflate the lower abdomen and then fill up the chest. Do not hold the breath, but gently, almost imperceptibly, change from inhalation to exhalation, letting the abdomen deflate first—to get rid of stale air at the bottom of the lungs—and then letting the air empty out of the chest. Exhale through the mouth until no more air comes out, but do not strain or force. Gently begin another inhalation, and continue the cycle for a few minutes.

2. Taoist Breathing

This second-stage practice is a little more difficult. At first, as you exhale through the mouth, imagine your Qi sinking down to the *Huiyin* point (on the perineum, at the base of the torso), and if you are standing bend the knees until the thighs are parallel to the ground (or as far as you are comfortable). Then lead the Qi down further, directing it through the thighs, the knees, the ankles, and all the way down to *Yongquan* point (in the arches of the feet just behind the big-toe joint). Then, as you inhale through the nose, reverse the course and lead the Qi back up to *Mingmen*. Repeat the down-and-up cycle for a few minutes.

3. Grabbing Hold of the Breath

This is the third stage of qi-gong breathing. Attempt it after you have mastered Taoist Breathing. Note that the directions given below assume you are standing, but it also fine if you wish to sit or to recline.

At the end of Taoist Breathing, exhale through the mouth and lead the Qi down to *Yongquan*, then desist from taking a breath for as long as is comfortable. Then, breathing in through the nose, lead the Qi back up through the ankles, thighs, perineum, and sacro-coccygeal area back up to *Mingmen* on the back of the waist. While inhaling, clench both hands into tight fists, grab the ground with the toes of both feet, touch the tongue to the ridge above the upper teeth, gently contract the anal sphincter, and breathe in until you cannot take in any more air. Then hold the breath for as long as is comfortable. Then, as you exhale through the mouth, completely relax the body and once again lead the Qi all the way down to *Yongquan*. Repeat the down-and-up cycle for a few minutes.

4. Breathing with the Throat and Mind

This fourth stage of qi-gong training is more subtle. Unlike the other forms, do not pay any attention as to whether you are breathing through your nose or your mouth. Use the mind to imagine that you are breathing, and feel the air as it passes through your throat. First, inhale very slowly and very deeply, and be very conscious of the inflow of Qi into your body. Allow the abdomen to inflate as always. The small act of willing yourself to breathe will strengthen and fill the extra Qi channel that flows around the waist, and from there you will be able to distribute it to any part of the body. You can "grab" the breath when you inhale, as in Exercise 3, or you can experiment with sending the Qi to various parts of your body as you exhale, or both, as you like. Repeat the exercise for a few minutes.

5. Mental Breathing

Exercise 5 is an even more advanced method of internal breathing. It is different from Exercise 4 in that whenever you have a need to send Qi to a certain part of the body, the Qi will flow there automatically. There is no correlation between breathing and movement in this exercise.

This type of breathing is very difficult to practice, but you might find it useful to focus on the *dantian* and to revolve the Qi around that area, first starting with small circles, gradually spiralling outward to larger circles. You should do this both clockwise and counterclockwise, performing the same number of circles in each direction.

Another exercise you can try—and one that does use the breath—is to fill the extra channel around the waist (*see* Fig. 16, p. 14) with Qi while inhaling, and then try to send the Qi to your extremities while exhaling.

Repeat the exercise for a few minutes.

6. Revolving Breath

Stand (or sit or recline) as in Exercise 3. As you inhale, send the Qi down the channel on the front of the body (*see* Fig. 14, p. 14), through the *dantian* and all the way down to the *Huiyin* point; then, as you exhale, send the Qi up the channel that runs along the back (*see* Fig. 13, p. 14), through the *Baihui* point on the crown of the head, and down the forehead to the mouth. As you inhale, continue the revolution of the Qi as before.

If you get good at this, you might benefit from trying to make the Qi flow in the same direction but against the breath—that is, as you exhale, send it down the front of the body, bringing it up the back and over the head as you inhale.

Or you might consider moving the Qi in the opposite direction—

that is, as you inhale, send it up over the head and down the back, and then bring it back up the front as you exhale.

Repeat this exercise, which will facilitate the easy flow of Qi throughout the body, for a few minutes.

7. Sinking Breath

This seventh type of breathing is not really the most difficult; in fact, it is sometimes used as a preparatory exercise. It is suitable for anyone, especially beginners, and is good for helping to alleviate such problems as hypertension, chronic fatigue, and insomnia.

First, get into any position that you find comfortable. Relax the mind and body, taking a few deep breaths if you like. This exercise will completely ignore the inhalation, which you may do in any manner you like, although abdominal breathing will be more beneficial.

Next, coordinate your mind with the exhalation. With each exhalation, lead the breath/Qi with the mind—imagining it even if you cannot feel it—down from *Mingmen* through the *dantian* to *Huiyin,* and further down through the thighs, knees, and ankles, to the arches and *Yongquan.* Some people say that the sinking of the breath with this exercise makes them feel as though the Qi is like a flow of warm air; others say it feels like a hot steam and actually makes them hot and causes them to sweat. Remember that no attention at all is paid to the inhaling of air, which should remain natural.

Repeat the exercise for a few minutes.

Conclusion

When you want to finish, take a few seconds to gradually stop the movement of the breath/Qi, and collect the body's Qi and store it in the *dantian.* Slowly open the eyes. Rub the hands together until they get hot, then rub the face, limbs, and trunk with them. Sit upright, or stand, and sink the breath with the mind down to the *Yongquan* point, then move about and walk around for a few minutes.

SELF-MASSAGE OF THE FIVE ORGANS

(Wuzang paozhi anmo)

The Self-Massage of the Five Organs exercises are more effective if they are preceded by one of the breathing exercises given earlier. They do not make up a continuous set that is practiced all at once, although they can be done in that manner if you like. Success at performing these exercises depends upon your ability to give off your own Qi, and also to send both internal and external Qi to the internal organs in order to strengthen them.

Below we have given some exercises that we feel will be useful in helping the organs to function better. When trying them, you may massage your skin, or you may wear clothes—it does not matter. Also, you may press down gently on the body, or keep the hands just out of contact with the body.

1. Heart Massage

1. Do a breathing exercise of your choice.
2. If male, put the left hand on the heart region just below the left breast, and place the right hand on top of the left. If you are female, reverse the hands.
3. Massage the area by making 12 counterclockwise and then 12 clockwise circles. Then take 3 deep breaths and exhale slowly. Press down with the palms when exhaling, and lift them up when inhaling. When massaging (and pressing), imagine that vital Qi is flowing from your hands to your heart.

This represents 1 round. Perform 3 rounds.

2. Liver Massage

1. Do a breathing exercise of your choice.
2. If male, put the left hand on the liver region just below the right ribs, and place the right hand on top of the left. If you are female, reverse the hands.
3. Massage the area by making 12 clockwise and then 12 counterclockwise circles. Then take 3 deep breaths and exhale slowly. Press down with the palms when exhaling, and lift them up when inhaling. When massaging (and pressing), imagine that vital Qi is flowing from your hands to your liver.

This represents 1 round. Perform 3 rounds.

3. Kidney Massage

1. Do a breathing exercise of your choice.
2. Place both hands on the kidney region on the lower back. Your fingertips should be near the *Shenshu* points (about 1.5 inches to either side of the spinous process of the second lumbar vertebra.
3. Massage the area by making 12 up-and-down motions and then 12 back-and-forth motions with the hands. Then take 3 deep breaths and exhale slowly. Press down with the palms when exhaling, and lift them up when inhaling. When massaging (and pressing), imagine that vital Qi is flowing from your hands to your kidneys.

This represents 1 round. Perform 3 rounds.

4. Lung Massage

1. Do a breathing exercise of your choice.
2. Place both palms over the lung region on your chest. (If you have a known problem, then place the hands over the problem area.)
3. Massage the area by making 12 circles inward and then 12 circles outward with the palms. Then take 3 deep breaths and exhale slowly. Press down with the palms when exhaling, and lift them up when inhaling. When massaging (and pressing), imagine that vital Qi is flowing from your hands to your lungs.

This represents 1 round. Perform 3 rounds.

5. Spleen and Stomach Massage

For treatment of splenomegaly (enlargement of the spleen) or dyspepsia, do the Spleen Massage. For treatment of thoracic depression, abdominal distension, gastric ulcer, or gastritis, do the Stomach Massage.

1. Do a breathing exercise of your choice.
2. *Spleen Massage:* If male, put the left hand on the "spleen" region just below the left ribs, and place the right hand on top of the left. If you are female, reverse the hands. Massage the area by making 12 counterclockwise and then 12 clockwise circles. Then take 3 deep breaths and exhale slowly. Press down with the palms when exhaling, and lift them up when inhaling. When massaging (and pressing), imagine that vital Qi is flowing from your hands to your liver.

This represents 1 round. Perform 3 rounds.

3. *Stomach Massage:* If male, put the left hand on the "stomach" region, putting the palm directly over the *Zhongwan* point (in the middle of the upper abdomen, halfway between the navel and the sternum), and place the right hand on top of the left. If you are female, reverse the hands. Massage the area by making 12 counterclockwise and then 12 clockwise circles. Then take 3 deep breaths and exhale slowly. Press down with the palms when exhaling, and lift them up when inhaling. When massaging (and pressing), imagine that vital Qi is flowing from your hands to your stomach.

This represents 1 round. Perform 3 rounds.

Finishing

Keep in mind when doing the exercises that you may increase the number of times you make circles and do the press-down breathing to any number you like. It will be easier if you increase the circles by multiples of 6, and try to keep the total of press-down breathing to about 25 percent of the number of circles made in one direction.

When you want to finish, do another breathing exercise of your choice; afterward, spend a few seconds to gradually stop the movement of the breath/Qi, then collect the body's Qi and store it between the *Mingmen* point and the *dantian*. Slowly open the eyes. Rub the hands together until they get hot, then rub the face, limbs, and trunk with them. Sit upright, or stand, and sink the breath with the mind down to the *Yongquan* point, then move about and walk around for a few minutes.

Conclusion

In closing, we hope that you have enjoyed learning more about Qigong and that the exercises you choose to practice will give you health and pleasure for many years to come.

Below is a summary of the exercises contained in this book, explaining their physical benefits. Please note the things to remember if you wish to get the most out of the effort you put into these exercises. You should also remember that the exercises in this book are not meant to describe a whole sequence of movements from beginning to end; rather, they are six different methods of gaining and maintaining health and promoting a longer and richer life.

Therefore, choose exercises according to your needs, and never strain; never go beyond your ability to do any movement to the point of discomfort or pain; always relax the body and mind thoroughly, and practice what you like at your own pace.

SUMMARY OF THE EXERCISES

Exercise	*Benefits*	*Note*
Warming-up Qigong (for everyone)	Good for circulation and general well-being.	Pay attention to the breathing, start the exercises slowly, and gradually increase the number.
Everyday Stretching Exercises (for everyone, especially good for adults)	Promote correct breathing, strengthen muscles, tendons, ligaments, and bones.	Each movement is a separate exercise; thus, you can do any you like in any order. Start with a few exercises and

Exercise	_Benefits_	_Note_
		gradually build up your own routine.
Life-Prolonging Qigong (for adults)	Relieve fatigue and relax both body and mind. Strengthen the muscles and increase flexibilty. Good for the internal organs. Help digestion and circulation.	Concentrate on doing the exercises smoothly. Relax while doing them, and coordinate the movements with the breath. Start with simple exercises and work up to more difficult ones.
13 Grand Preservers (for older adults)	Promote circulation and improve co-ordination. Help relieve stiffness in muscles and joints. Keep the neck, shoulders, waist, lower back, and legs relaxed but conditioned, and give some relief from arthritis and internal disorders.	Take your time in learning the movements. Not a set of vigorous movements, it is suited to the elderly. Exercise slowly and in coordination with the breath.
Breathing Exercises (for everyone)	Improve the circulation of both blood and Qi, and increase general vitality. Purify the entire system.	Relax both the body and the mind when doing any of these exercises. Do not be too anxious to get on to the next exercise or your other business, and do not expect to receive benefits right away. Try to exercise in a place with fresh air, and be careful not to breathe too deeply.
Self-massage of the Five Organs (for adults)	Help to alleviate and prevent tension. Build up resistance to disease. Increase the efficiency of blood circulation.	You can gain the greatest benefit by doing these exercises either just after getting up or just before going to bed.